CHICO
LIFE AND TIMES OF
A CITY OF FORTUNE

The Chico Electric Railway Company was organized in 1904 to provide streetcar transportation to the growing town of Chico and the surrounding area. (Courtesy of Meriam Library Special Collections.)

CHICO

LIFE AND TIMES OF A CITY OF FORTUNE

DEBRA MOON

ARCADIA

First printed 2003.
Reprinted 2004, 2005.

Published by Arcadia Publishing
Charleston SC, Chicago IL, Portsmouth NH, San Francisco CA

Printed in Great Britain.

Library of Congress Catalog Card Number: 2003108744

For all general information contact Arcadia Publishing at:
Telephone 843-853-2070
Fax 843-853-0044
E-Mail sales@arcadiapublishing.com
For customer service and orders:
Toll-Free 1-888-313-2665

Visit us on the Internet at http://www.arcadiapublishing.com

CONTENTS

ACKNOWLEDGMENTS

I have found the information for this account of Chico's history by sifting through histories of Butte County, the Bidwells, Northern California, California Natives, and by interviewing people who remember parts of Chico's past. The works of Dorothy Hill, regarding the Mechoopda Tribe of the Chico area, were especially interesting and thorough. She spent time personally interviewing and recording information from the local tribe.

An enjoyable part of my work has been the personal interviews I conducted for original research on Chico's past. True to the town's reputation, Chico citizens have been open and generous in offering their own collections of historical documentation, their time, and their memories. In this brief synopsis, I could not possibly include all the detailed stories of development and human interaction that makes up Chico history.

The family of Benjamin Schuyster Kerns, now living mostly in Klamath Falls, Oregon, was a particularly memorable surprise. I thank them for their cooperation and generosity, and for the touching video they sent depicting the story of Chico's famous young aviator, Thadeus Kerns.

There are different versions of history, and not all facts are recorded accurately. I am a newspaper photojournalist, and I can vouch that newspaper accounts are surprisingly accurate, considering the speed at which they are produced, but sacrifices are made to meet ever-present deadlines. News articles are often the only source of written history, even for important events.

I would like to thank my daughter Jennifer for her endless editing help, and the rest of my family for their general support of my writing efforts.

As for citizens of Chico, I would like to thank Steve Santos, chairman of the Mechoopda Tribe; the lovely Frances Mathews, for her videos and photo albums; Ann Sigel, for her husband's clippings, brochures, and city council records, which provided much needed documentation; and Chip Meriam, for his trust and efficiency in providing information from the more recent past. The King family was extremely supportive and encouraging. I want to thank Ann and Tony Sands for their memories, stories, and their big stash of news articles. I appreciate John Nopel's guidance and direction. I appreciate the help of Mick Needham, of long-time Chico business Needham's Stained Glass, with some detailed local railroad information. Thanks are due as well to Mike Hicks and Darrell Deter for digging up old photos and sharing family stories. I also appreciate time spent by Fred Davis, Matt Livingston, and the crew at the U.S. Forest Service Genetic Resource and Conservation Center, known locally as the "Tree Farm."

I cannot thank everyone who helped, so I will have to say that this was a community effort in many ways, and I'd like to thank everyone who offered their time and knowledge. It was another Chico accomplishment.

Chapter One

A SKETCH OF CHICO

The prevailing image of Chico is of an established community with broad, tree-lined streets, laced by cool, shaded streams, surrounded on the north, west, and south by luxuriant orchards, and nestled at the base of the Sierra Nevada foothills. In this sense, Chico's rural image depends on the close affinity its residents feel with the immediately surrounding countryside, the relatively comprehensible scale of the community, and the physical integration of the natural environment into the urban fabric.

–City of Chico General Plan, 1990

Chico today is a thriving town of 100,000 people, comfortably settled on the Sacramento Valley floor, north of Sacramento, the state capital of California. The projected population of the city by the year 2010 is 138,000. It is the home of a university campus, the California State University at Chico, and is the fastest growing community in Butte County, possibly even in northern California. Investors and would-be homeowners come from the San Francisco Bay Area, and other locations, to find refuge in Chico's pleasant tree-lined streets.

East of Chico, the western slopes of the Sierra Nevadas catch moisture-laden winds. The climate and soil have produced stands of timber and nurtured many years of agriculture. Profitable gold mining took place near Chico. Other precious stones and minerals, diamonds, chrome, uranium, coal, and some copper were also found there.

The city is located 90 miles northwest of Sacramento and 180 miles northeast of San Francisco. The Rancheria of the Mechoopda Indians was in the center of the land that was purchased by John Bidwell, the founder of the city. Chico is on an alluvial fan, sloping broadly from the foothills to the Sacramento River. It was formed by deposits from the Big and Little Chico Creeks to the north, and the Lindo Channel, where it diverts from the Big Chico Creek, runs for 6 miles in a westward direction, then rejoins the Chico Creek 3 miles east of the confluence with the Sacramento River. The channel creates a marshland, which adds an interesting dimension to the ecosystems. To the south of Little Chico Creek, there are the Big and Little Butte Creeks. Along these streams are volcanic rock and soil, and fossils in sandstone mixed with the alluvial deposits.

Chico is 210 feet above sea level. Its climate is hot and dry, with an average of 23.56 inches of rain annually. The average temperature over a period of 61 years was 62.5, with a range from approximately 35 degrees in winter to 98.4 in summer. Highs and lows have reached further extremes.

The enduring resources for Chico have proven to be land and water. The soil, and the Sacramento River and its tributaries, have sustained a variety of life. The Sacramento River is sometimes called the western Mississippi, and Chico is located only 7 miles from its banks. River landings were important for trade and transportation, for natives of the area and the early settlers.

The city's fortune began with the Sacramento River and the life it brought to the area. It was rich in flora and fauna. Then white settlers discovered conventional riches in the form of gold and other minerals. Seekers of fortune assembled in the Sacramento Valley to strike it rich and opportunists soon followed. They made their money catering to the gold miners and quickly relieving them of the gold they'd just obtained. This is an often-repeated story for many California towns of the era. However, Chico's fortune extended to something beyond the material. A spirit of generosity and unselfishness has hallmarked the city. There are a considerable number of tales and legacies of special individuals who demonstrated sacrifice and thoughtfulness. The native residents, the Mechoopda, were exceptionally responsive, helpful, and hard-working individuals. The early settlers, unusually civic-minded, were somewhat hand-picked by John Bidwell and other leaders. Before California statehood, John Bidwell became the landowner of a tract of land that was the land grant, Rancho Chico, and gave or sold land to people he thought would make good community citizens. The city of Chico was laid out on this land; lots were donated for the city plaza, churches, clinics, and community agencies and organizations. Steve Santos, present day chairman of the Mechoopda tribe says, "There is something special about this area that people are drawn to. They come to school here, and then seek desperately to stay. There is a community feeling."

The fortunes of Chico today are its environmental resources, its people, its economic strength, and an abiding atmosphere of relaxation and serenity. The sense of community was forged deliberately by far-sighted and unselfish people whose actions seemed to prevail before the actual founding of the city, and for years to follow, as Chico society formed. Today Chico residents enjoy the contributions and sacrifices made by these dynamic people of Chico's past. In many ways, Chico is a City of Fortune.

Chapter Two

ORIGINAL INHABITANTS OF THE CHICO AREA

The banks of the Sacramento River, first seen by native inhabitants of the northern central valley of California, are thousands of years old. It is the longest river in California, 380 miles, or 612 kilometers, in length. Like most large rivers in the nation, it serves at the present time as a source of electricity and irrigation water, yet it radiates a sense of history, wholeness, and integrity. This river is unique. In 1945, the Shasta Dam, dividing the upper river and lower river, was completed. Although the northern portion is more wild and active, the southern portion, (the focus of this history) is peaceful, languid, and rich. In its presence one might feel a power of healing, and that certainly is satisfying and nurturing. It has been called many names by various native groups, including Bohema-mem, or Great Water, but it is no surprise the name used by Hispanic settlers prevailed. It is the Rio de Sacramento, or River of the Blessed Sacrament.

Before any European settlers saw the river, it was the site of ancient, native villages. There were an estimated 1,000 inhabitants of these "Korusi" villages along the Sacramento River in the area in 1850. There were at least 13 original villages recorded in history, and probably many more weren't mentioned. By 1900, only two of these ancient villages remained, and not one exists today.

The river was a source of plentiful wildlife, plant life, and water supply that natives depended on to sustain their lives and care for their families. The natives were stewards of the valley and foothill areas, nurturing food resources by controlled hunting and grass burnings. They built warm and comfortable shelters. As these groups thrived and prospered in the area, more native settlements or communities appeared scattered on the land farther from the river. The people who populated these communities in or around the Chico area spoke a Maidu dialect and considered themselves to be associated with other Maidu communities.

The ancient people along the river were called "Kuksu" or "Big-Head Dancers" by the Maidu because of the headdresses they wore for ceremonial dances. They began the celebration of life events for the people, setting the traditions for dances and ceremonies to celebrate harvest, the change of season, births, deaths, and the coming of manhood and womanhood. Some ceremonies were also in commemoration of the dead. Traditions and ceremonies characteristic of native Maidu, and other groups, were born in these ancient villages located on, or near, the river. The influence of the Kuksu reached to the Valley Maidu, the River Patwin, Pomo, Clear Lake and Russian River villages, the Sacramento Valley, and Coastal Range areas of California.

The natives in the Chico area identified strongly with their own small band or community. They are Maidu but, more accurately, they are from the Mechoopda village. Dorothy Hill, Chico resident and descendent of an early settler, J.J. Morehead, wrote her dissertation on the Mechoopda people, and she referred to them as a "tribelet." They were part of a northwestern Maidu group. At first they lived from the area of what today is called Dayton to the east side of Little Chico Creek. When John Bidwell, an early Chico pioneer, bought the Mexican land grant, Rancho Chico, from William Dickey, the Mechoopda were Bidwell's most immediate neighbors.

CHICO

The Mechoopda Rancheria originally had several villages and many affiliations with other "tribelets" in the area. During ceremonies they were often joined by Maidu from Oroville and Konkau (today called Concow), and by Wintun and Yana nearby. The older village of the Mechoopda was called Paki, Paiki, or Paihkem. This may have been the village John Bidwell made note of in his writings. It was located on lower Little Chico Creek, west of the confluence of Mud Creek with Big Chico Creek. C. Hart Meriam also wrote about this village in 1923. This was the first Mechoopda hulhli, or village, 5 miles east of Chico and 3 miles northeast of Durham. The summer camp for the Mechoopda was set up on the south bank of the Big Chico Creek and was called Chulamsewi.

Other villages bordered Big Chico Creek, the Lindo Channel, and Pine Creek. In the late 1830s, the Mechoopda had located their village on the southeast bank of the Big Chico Creek, a small tributary to the Sacramento River flowing out of the foothills and through what is now the city of Chico and the university in the downtown area. It was located near what is now First and Flume Streets.

All native people in California, before the arrival of the Europeans, lived in small villages, each with a population somewhere in the proximity of 100 persons. The Mechoopda were no exception. Their villages recognized a tract of land as their own and some outlying resources as theirs. The tribe shared resources with other communities, for example the river, hunting territories, or salt mining areas. Less likely to be shared were stands of oaks, which were shepherded and cared for by the people of the community, and therefore more of a territorial resource. There were areas of "no man's land," which were travel corridors.

The Mechoopda lived, gathered food, and hunted the majority of the time in a 6-mile radius from their home. They could comfortably walk in this area and return home in a day's travel. This circle was part of another 12-mile radius where further hunting and gathering took place on a more seasonal basis. These trips were planned and prepared for in advance, and entailed overnight or several day journeys to obtain some foods or materials for tools, clothing, or building. There were forays into the environment, which were of a longer distance. According to Dorothy Hill's account, the Mechoopda contained themselves to a 20-mile radius of varied ecosystems, in which they found all they needed.

The five ecosystems available to the Mechoopda in this 20-mile radius, described in Dorothy Hill's treatise on the Indians of the Chico Rancheria, were: grasslands, foothills, streamside woodlands, marshlands, and yellow pine stands. In the streamside woodlands the Indians found wild grapes, acorns, fresh water clams and mussels, perch and salmon, and sometimes pacific eel. They also used oaks, alders, sycamores, and willows for raw materials. The grasslands provided the Indians with deer, elk, antelope, grizzlies, hemp, poppies, rabbits, and grasshoppers. The marshlands gave them geese, mallards, tule grass, stream leaves, and other materials. The foothills were a source of basketry materials and various types of game. At a higher elevation the Indians found nuts and foods in the form of roots and plants as well as larger game.

The villages most often consisted of a few households of blood relatives. However, several of these would be scattered in close geographical vicinity to others, with one site that was the "main village" or mother village. New sub-settlements might be inhabited, abandoned, or re-inhabited. Several villages of one dialect may have a recognized chief or leader; however, this person did not hold comprehensive governing authority. Communities had their own experts, leaders, families of authority, or elders of authority for most purposes. Various individuals in the group would be appointed to lead in different facets of life, including: spiritual or moral issues, dealing with spirits of the dead or possessive spirits and illnesses, visions and discerning the future, hunting or procuring food, protection, healing and medicine, negotiations within the village or with other villages, or the ceremonial calendar, among other things.

For the valley Maidu, the chieftain of the tribe, or headman, was a hereditary position from a male line of descent, but there were exceptions. Sometimes a distinguished person, a healer or fighter, could be considered a leader, or a poor one could be deposed at the will of the group. They were usually phased out, rather than deposed, to save face. The names natives assigned to the leaders, or to a village, normally only meant "people" in their own language. Sometimes names were more descriptive, meaning a certain kind of people or those of a certain place. Occasionally these designations were humorous, such as "The Flea People," "The People Who Live on the Sand," or "The Grass-Eaters."

The concept of "tribe" may have applied to other native groups in our nation from the East or Midwest. It is likely, though, that European traders and settlers, who were eager to negotiate terms and use the lands and resources of the groups, also imposed this concept in those areas. Certainly, the federal government, Russia, and Mexico sought "tribal leaders" for contracts and treaty signings. In reality, that was not how the governance of the native people worked. The autonomy of these groups was highly inconvenient to newcomers seeking to use resources or settle in the area. Not having an understanding of the culture or language, newcomers tended to group the people according to their own criteria, not by how the natives wanted. Joseph McGie in *History of Butte County* comments, "The Maidu did not consider themselves a homogenous group or 'nation.' They were not always well understood by each other."

Natives who were here, or who remain, and still know the story, have written little about their history. Most recorded information is from Europeans, most of whom did not speak native dialects. According to European observations at the time, it was thought that the western limit of the Maidu "territory" was the Sacramento River. The eastern boundary appeared to be Honey Lake, in what is now Lassen County.

Some accounts and research conducted by settlers and scholars have been deemed quite accurate. Also, and fortunately, for historical purposes, many interviews have been conducted with native groups and individuals in the past 100 years that leave a more accurate depository of information on life as the original residents knew it. Dorothy Hill performed interviews with Mechoopda natives that have shed light on details of their culture, beliefs, and history. Some very important Mechoopda natives assisted her: Tom Epperson, Amanda Wilson, Henry Azbill, Mabel Baker, and others.

A few Mechoopda men and women, and some Maidus, working in the school systems and the community, have attempted to share what was passed down to them to keep the knowledge of their native culture alive. Amanda Wilson, a Mechoopda from the northwest settlement, and Pablo Sylvers, a Wintun from Tehama, who considered himself "almost" Mechoopda, were also helpful in passing the culture on.

Marie Potts, a Maidu born near Lake Almanor in 1885 at Big Meadow, founded the oldest native newspaper, *Smoke Signal*. It dealt with the Indians' struggle for their rights and presented important aspects of their culture. Her Indian name was Chankutpan, meaning, "One with Sharp Eyes." She put herself through Carlisle Indian School in Pennsylvania, graduating in 1942. She then began to teach Indian history and culture in the Sacramento schools. Another Maidu who shared her culture was Mary Jones, of Willows, a teacher who showed basket weaving and design, and other things about Maidu, to classes in the area.

Frank Day, a contemporary Maidu artist, expressed many of his cultural beliefs through art. His Indian name was "ly dam lily," meaning "fading morning star." He was born in Butte County in 1902, and his father was Konkau Maidu. His art depicts primitive concepts and scenes. The work has been displayed in several galleries in Chico, Oroville, Davis, Folsom, San Francisco, and Washington, D.C. His work stayed longest at the Sacramento Crocker Art Gallery in California. When Frank Day died in 1977, the Maidu did not perform ceremonies for one entire year in his honor.

All travelers through the north central valley of California, in the last half of the 1800s, agreed that the native groups in the mountain areas seemed to be more aggressive. Few estimates exist on the population of the mountain villages, and what has been recorded is probably not accurate. Conflicts did occur between groups. They were usually over food supply, territory, or migration. When fighting was necessary, weapons were used, including slings, spears, arrows, stones, and clubs. Attack usually occurred at daybreak when two lines of warriors gesticulating, shouting insults, and careening about shooting arrows, would meet.

The Maidus and the Patwins often attended each other's ceremonies. There was intermarriage between villages, and less often, between what we now call "tribes." Trading and other interactions took place between communities, but in the days of the original inhabitants of the land it was possible that a person from one community could live an entire lifetime without meeting more than 200 other persons. The valley Maidu traded items, such as smoked salmon, bows, and arrows with the "mountain" people and other tribes.

Records of tribes and names of groups varied greatly between individuals, and the population was changing rapidly in size and location in the mid-1800s. Walton E. Bean, in his 1937 publication *California, an Interpretive History*, paints a tragic picture of the changing population:

> In 1789 the Indian population was 275,000 with a few dozen Spaniards, Americans and a few thousand Mexican-Californians. By 1846 epidemics and other factors had decimated the Indian population to 100,000. By 1870, there were estimated 30,000 Indians, in 1900, fewer than 16,000 Indians remained in the state—starvation, malnutrition added to the toll as the Indians were driven from their food producing areas.

According to research, the whites in the valley introduced malaria in 1831, or possibly before. The disease decimated many natives before the gold rush even started. Once the gold rush began, it brought so many whites that the inevitable conflict over land, safety, and food supply ensued. The natives were largely displaced without any negotiations at all. Along with this displacement and interruption of the food supply, the natives suffered more disease and personal conflicts, which eventually led to their round up and march out of the Sacramento Valley.

This tragedy was the northern California version of events that were taking place across the nation and were a regrettable part of the story of United States expansion. In Chico, it seemed even more of a deplorable misfortune because of the nature of the Mechoopda.

Native residents of the Chico area were a people of great gentleness and consideration. They lived a communal life and had a cooperative spirit. They demonstrated ingenuity and extensive knowledge of factors in the local environment, particularly soil, water, minerals, weather, plants, and animals. They had highly developed skills and a complex language. The customs and daily life of the Mechoopda were drastically different from the Spanish, the Mexicans, and white settlers who began to populate their land.

The men of the Mechoopda society were observed to have soft fine beards and, in general, they went naked. In cold weather, they wore a protective coating of mud, or possibly a cape made of deer hide or feathers. In winter, they wore well-made moccasins with a center seam running from the big toe along the instep to the base of the shin. The moccasins were made of deer hide with the hair left on for protection from snow. Grasses were placed inside, at the bottom, as insulation. There were wrap-around leggings from ankle to knee. Robes were made by sewing six or seven bobcat skins together, with the hair left on them. At all times of the year, they might have painted their faces, or marked them with a tar-like substance. This may have been to protect them from spirits or worldly dangers. Cloth was unknown to the California Indians, who instead wove mats together or feathers into a feather blanket from cords or strips of duck skins.

The women often wore tattoos. The design could distinguish their lineage or village, or both. They were generally tattooed below the mouth. They wore a summer clothing apron of tule grasses or the shredded bark of willow trees. The grass skirt hung from their waist to their knees, in front and back, and was open at the sides. Sometimes they wore leaves or flowers on their heads.

Early settlers termed the peaceful valley natives "diggers" because worms, insects, and roots that they dug from the ground were part of their diet. This was a particularly derogatory name and did not give credit to the original Chico inhabitants for their fishing and hunting skill, their calendar, their mercantile aptitude, their basket-weaving skills, their conservation practices, or their religious faith.

The Mechoopda and other Maidu wore necklaces of shells traded with coastal tribes. Earrings were also made from bird wings or bird leg bones adorned with brightly colored quail or woodpecker feathers. Men wore flickertail headdresses during ceremonies. Some had over 5,000 flicker feathers and measured over 2 feet long and up to 5 inches high. They wore woven feather quilts. They tattooed their arms and upper body with red and white clay and black charcoal. The designs were made of slash marks and dots.

The Mechoopda religion established a well-run society with orderly observance and accommodations of events in the lives of the village members. They believed in "Ko-doyapen," a mother Supreme Being, who ran the universe. The storms, wind, rain, and snow were believed to carry the voice of this being. They considered the earth to be round, and floating in water, tied by cord in five cardinal directions: north, northwest, south, west, and east. They believed that at death, spirits leave the body, but hover around for a period of time. These spirits might enter into the taboo animals, coyotes, bears, or snakes, or they might enter a rock, lake, or rainbow. The rainbow represented a benevolent spirit. Their religion was one of warding off evil. Dancing ceremonies and tattooing the body were for this purpose.

There is an elaborate set of legends, including creation of the earth, the entrance of evil into the world through the trickster Coyote, and even a flood story where the whole earth is covered in water, and only a big canoe full of people and animals is saved, which drifts to Canoe Mountain where it finally settles, high and dry.

The white deer was sacred and was said to be seen in the Sutter Buttes. Indeed natives did have white deerskins, specially decorated and painted for ceremony. The "Hesi" was, and still is, the main dance of the Kuksu. It is done in October and May. It was performed in the Marysville Buttes, and was an occasion for different villages to get together to pool resources for a big feast and celebration, in the spirit of the pow-wow today. In the Hesi Circle the "deer people" danced and sweated, and four songs were sung. A full-feathered cloak was used for the Hesi ceremonies and revolved around 14 spirits, some of more importance than others. The Duck was very important; the Grizzly Bear and Deer ranked next, and then the Coyote and Goose.

On a daily basis, the Mechoopda greeted the sunrise with a prayer of thankfulness as well one at the end of day after washing. This thankfulness also extended to game they caught, and they gave it back to the earth, and to plants for using them for sustenance. Each time they took food, they left gifts of acorn meal, tobacco, or other foodstuffs in thanks.

Mechoopda dances were the oldest form of folklore. The chants and movements told a story in a pageantry of prayer. Tribal members danced for rain, for good crops, for well being, and to appease the spirits. Their dances made good medicine to stave off evil spirits that bring sickness and suffering.

The Bear Dance was held in the spring when the first edible shoots came through the ground. Previous to this big event, the women had a "pow-wow," a get-together to grind acorns. Fish and game that had been caught by the men were prepared for the feast. Food was shared with all families. Anything leftover was divided among the people and taken home in baskets. Although the dances are not performed exactly like they had been in ancient times, they still are done from time to time. The White Deer and other dances are said to be especially significant in the modern era.

The marriage customs were simple. First the young man visited often. If he was acceptable, they took him in as son-in-law with no barter. A young man would move in with his bride's family. There was a period of servitude, which is common even amongst tribal people today. Once this period was over, he could take her to their own household. There was no formal marriage ceremony.

The Mechoopda had distinctly unusual burial customs. When a person died, the body was dressed as nicely as possible in some of the deceased's best clothing, or gifts of clothing given by friends and relatives for the burial occasion. The body was then bent into a fetal position, tied with a cord, as well as wrapped first in a net, then in perhaps a bearskin, or maybe more than one when possible. The grave was one-and-a-half meters deep, placed near the village to prevent the raiding of graves for beads and precious items by other groups or wanderers. Bark was placed over the body before putting dirt into the grave. The body was buried facing west.

Once laid to rest, the widows cut their hair and covered their head, neck, and breast with pine pitch, nutmeg, or peppermint. They were never allowed to wash this off, it had to wear off naturally over a period of a year or more. If it came off too soon, watchful relatives added more.

The men might also cut their hair and might wear pitch, too, and refrain from joining in their normal activities, such as gambling or dancing, until after the "burn." A burning ground was part of every village. It would normally be located on a rise, which was not covered with brush. A date would be set for the burning, and all those appropriate would be invited. As was the custom of many other natives at the time, the invitees would be given a string with knots tied in to help calculate the date of the upcoming event. One knot was for every day between the time the string was given and the date of the burning. Attendance was "paid for" with beads. The village it was set for would provide the food for all those coming. A warm-up ceremony would be held the day before, and there would be crying at the graves, as well as laying of flour (edible) and earth over the final resting spot. Some people made images to be burned. At dusk these images, along with gifts, were placed on top of poles with huge piles of brush leaning against them. The Shaman would receive the beads paid by everyone present and he would begin the crying. Others would soon join in and this would continue through the night until sunrise.

Although the burial customs of the Mechoopda were difficult for white settlers to accept, their medical practices and cures were sometimes sought. The Mechoopda were very resourceful and made medicine from roots, bark, leaves, herbs, fruit, and blossoms. Women could administer the common or easily obtainable ingredients. Only the Medicine Men could administer the medicine that was rare or from far away.

Original Inhabitants of the Chico Area

Jimson Weed or Datura had many uses for the Mechoopda. In addition to being a cure for debility, it was used for producing a religious frenzy, bordering on a narcotic state in ceremonies. Datura was given for anesthesia or when bones had to be set. It was an aphrodisiac and was also good luck when gambling.

Tobacco was used in several ways. The sharing of tobacco in ceremonies was important. It was also given as a gift in payment for the services of a medicine man or other leader of the village. Tobacco was said to be cultivated and grown by northwestern groups, including the Yurok.

The Mechoopda used all they had available for curing disease and strengthening the weak amongst them. Unfortunately, there was not a good knowledge of physiology or anatomy. Some surgery was practiced, but it not on a regular basis. Bones were set, and there was knowledge of dentistry, limited basically to tooth extraction. Bloodletting was done to relieve pain and swelling. Pharmaceutical processes included percolation, leaching, and extraction. Decoctions and infusions were known and used. Immunizations, and later quarantine, were practiced. The Mechoopda had knowledge of the therapeutic effects of drugs, and the natural drugs they used were equal to those of contemporary white men in effectiveness and variety.

There were a number of Maidu dialects spoken in California; Mechoopda most resembles the KonKau Maidu. Some common words from the Mechoopda and Maidu dialects are encountered today. The valley Maidu called the land, or valley, "koyo." The word "sewi" means stream, "omo" was the word for people, and "konkau" for a large group of people. Today there is a town 25 miles from Chico named Concow, obviously derived from the Maidu word, "konkau."

The local natives, as well as many groups and tribes across the nation, were strict conservationists when it came to the use of natural resources. They did not believe in mining or disturbing the earth. A Maidu flint miner at Table Mountain, a mesa-like mountain about 14 miles southeast of Chico, was only permitted to take away as much flint as he could detach with a single blow of his hammer.

The Mechoopda were conservative hunters. Deer were plentiful and were taken with a bow and arrow. The hunter disguised himself with a deerskin and antlers as he crawled through grass to get close to the herd; he then thanked the herd for offering a member to feed the people. No more deer were killed than needed.

The Maidu were thriving in the Sacramento Valley before the arrival of white settlers who interrupted their food supply. The Mechoopda were expert shepherds of the many oak trees in the valley, and they had invented ways of storing the acorns and using them through winter. They had a variety of methods of cooking the nuts, which were their staple, and many ways of enlivening the flavor and texture. They were resourceful and wise in using and sustaining their food supply.

Acorns, roots, grass, seeds, and berries were eaten raw or cooked. A powder was made of the acorns by pounding them on large stones, after shelling and drying. The California Indian Museum reports that an Indian family would consume 1,000 to 2,000 pounds of acorns in a year. The acorn meal was leached with hot water and cooked before eaten. Until the settlers invaded the valley, acorns were plentiful and easy to obtain. Strange as it seems, the California Indians would not rob the woodpecker, except in times of extreme hunger. Stored neatly in separate holes in tree trunks, the woodpecker's acorns were respected by the Indians unless desperate measures were needed. Settlers reported the coarse acorn bread to be like "black clay," although it was sometimes flavored with berries and herbs. Some whites found the bread good to eat, with a texture like cheese.

The Mechoopda built granaries to store all the acorns they would need during the winter months. They were masters at constructing appropriate structures from materials in the environment, as well as designing them for ease, convenience, and protection from varmints and the elements.

CHICO

An acorn storage granary was called a "chuckah." This may have been a Miwok or Pomo term. It was built off the ground, above a boulder or tree stump. Poles would be placed in a circle around the outside of the tree stump. A grapevine, or some long willow branches, would be twined around the poles to make a rough, open container. Branches of willow, deer brush, or white fir were placed vertically, tip end down, in the twined circles to make a thatched wall. Then branches were tramped down from the inside, adding more and more branches, making a tighter thatch. Inside, the large container would be lined with wormwood and pine needles, repelling insects and keeping weather out, and holding the acorns from falling through. A helper on the outside handed things to the inside builder. Finally, the helper began to hand in acorns. When more were needed, they could be taken out of storage from the outside. Standing near the wall, the wormwood and pine needles were moved away to let the acorns flow from the chuckah into a basket held below the opening of the granary silo. When the basket was full, the wormwood and pine needles were replaced to protect the remaining acorns. This preparation required that the granaries be stocked with a two-year supply.

Grasshoppers were cleverly "harvested" by the Mechoopda, who found them to be good and plentiful food. The people dug pits into which the insects were driven by setting fire to the grass, or by beating the grass in a circle that got smaller and smaller with a pit in the center. Once driven into the pit, whose sides were smooth, steep, and deep, the grasshoppers could not escape. Clumps of grass lit on fire were tossed into the pits. The grasshoppers smothered in the smoke, and were then soaked in water and baked in ovens. A paste was made and eaten with the fingers, or a mush was made of the grasshopper powder. These insects were a delicacy and were dried for winter use. It was this that proved to be a favorite of John Bidwell.

The Maidu caught and ate fish, most of the time by either by spearing or netting. When a fish became caught in the net, it was easily brought in. Spears or javelins were 4 or 5 feet long, made of tough wood with heads of flint, bone, or obsidian (volcanic glass). They had movable heads attached to the shaft by a line so that the pole would serve as a float when the fish was hit. Another method was to stun the fish by putting turkey mullein or soap root plants in the water. When the Indians would put the plants in the stream the fish became immobile from the plants' effect, and the anglers quickly gathered up their stupefied reward.

The Maidu often worked cooperatively to secure food. In times of great need, they herded deer over cliffs to their death. Rabbit and small game were netted. Ducks were taken in large manmade nests constructed over the top of the marshes. Salmon were speared using dear horn attached to a cord. The Maidu also did bolo hunting. Certain foods were forbidden, such as coyote, dog, bear, buzzards, rattlesnake, and amphibians in general, because of religious and cultural beliefs.

Maidu dances and ceremonies began in October and ended in June. Winter was for staying home and summer was for travel. Daily life consisted of making a morning and evening meal at home and snacking in between. The Mechoopda made and repaired equipment on a daily basis. They went hunting and fishing and gathered food daily. Cooking and preparing food also took time daily. The young and the old worked. At night stories were told. It was considered bad luck to tell stories during the daylight hours.

Maidu homes varied from locality and season. In the mountains, shelters were sturdier, but in general they were all similar. Maidu Round Houses, found in Chico, were semi-subterranean lodges, partially dug down into the ground. The top part was a low mound covered with branches and mud. Round Houses stood 15 to 25 feet in diameter, and 10 to 15 feet high. Bathhouses were made of bent willow sticks, which formed a frame. Skins or rushes formed the cover. Heated rocks from the campfire were placed in the center and water was sprinkled over the hot rocks to make steam. This cleansing process loosened mud, mourning paint, or other dirt on the body. The skin was rubbed with moss or sticks to loosen dirt after a good steaming. The participants would then jump into cold water in a nearby stream.

The Mechoopda had hot weather camps. They often built awning structures near the house for additional shade and a working or resting space. Moving from one camp to another was not easy and took planning and good weather. Transportation down the rivers and streams was done by boat. Boats were bunches of rushes tied together with strong vines and were powered by the Mechoopda with wooden paddles. Snowshoes were used for overland travel in the winter.

In the daily life of the Mechoopda, there was time for games, toys, and amusements, just as there is in modern life. Mechoopda mothers made grass or bark dolls and doll baby baskets for their children. Teenage girls enjoyed football (soccer), and they played together with the boys. The girls did all the throwing, while the boys kicked the ball through the goal. A soccer game was played with a ball of skin stuffed with deer hair. The object was to force the ball through a line of opposing players.

The Grass Game was played at celebrations, especially in the mountain villages, and is now played at tribal get-togethers. Each player has a black and a white bone or pebble, which he hides in his hand under the grass. There are two teams of six players each. The opponents try to guess which hand holds the bone. Songs and drums accompany the game. Rhythms are beaten out with sticks, which adds to the excitement if a player makes a correct guess. If the guess is correct, the team scores one of six counters. The winning team must get all six before a new game starts.

Mechoopda natives excelled at basket weaving. Baskets were made of root fibers so finely woven that they could hold water or hot liquid food. They were used as fish traps, burden baskets, and held a variety of other uses. For instance, babies were kept in baskets, which were used like cradleboards.

Mechoopda craftsmanship could also be observed in their tools, such as stone and bone awls, obsidian arrowheads, spear point hooks, cutting stones, mortars, and metates. They made bows and arrows of local plants, stones, and feathers. They made fire drills of rosewood, with charcoal and grass in the bedplates.

The way of life for the Mechoopda in the Sacramento Valley was prescribed, as they had known it. It was sacred, and it was important to keep life in balance. Meanwhile, others discovered the area; before John Bidwell saw the land that would become Chico, white settlers had come through, and some were settling in the surrounding area. Reportedly, the first non-native person in the area was Gabriel Moraga.

The Mission Dolores, established in San Francisco in 1776, sent a soldier, Gabriel Moraga, in 1808 to try and find a site for an additional inland mission. He and a group of soldiers came up the American River to the canyons in the Sierras. They camped on the lower Feather River. Moraga is credited with naming the Sacramento River. He did not find a site for an inland mission, probably due to lack of suitable access. On the journey, Moraga met the Maidu. Although he never did set foot on the soil of the Arroyo Chico (Chico Creek), he did explore the general area around the Sutter Buttes and possibly came within 30 miles of what is Chico today. His descriptions of the area are very accurate. The early California historian, Rolland Dixon, mentions a Franciscan Father, Padre Abella, who reportedly had contact with the Maidu in the Sacramento Valley around 1811.

In the late 1820s, approximately 1827, Jedediah Smith and a group of frontier trappers came through the Sacramento Valley. Jedediah was a famous trapper passing through the area, no doubt hunting and ultimately headed for Oregon. He was the first American fur trapper to travel through Butte County.

He had 18 men with him and 315 horses, which he planned to trade to individual trappers for more furs. At this time California was under the rule of Mexico, not Spain. The Mexicans had ordered the Americans out of California, but Jedediah Smith was determined to explore the Sacramento River and the valley. He was interested in the great numbers of beaver in the river and its tributaries. At that time, beaver hats were in great demand. Smith's diaries indicate that on January 28, 1828, he was following trails when he ran into the Mechoopda Indians.

The Hudson Bay Company, a large outfit of fur trappers, was in the area in 1831. This was unfortunate for the natives since these men brought diseases with them, which killed many of the Maidu. Captain Wilkes, a traveler and explorer in the area, noted that a population of 12,000 to 15,000 Indians along the Sacramento River had been reduced to 8,000 or 9,000 in his time. Malaria, cholera, smallpox, typhoid, pneumonia, influenza, and tuberculosis were reported ailments that many Indians died from.

In the early 1840s, after the numbers of the natives were much reduced, John Bidwell made many trips up the Sacramento River doing business of one kind or another. He was friendly with the Mechoopda, enjoyed their food and company, and negotiated business with them. Paul Roberts, of the *Chico Record*, in the late 1880s wrote that Bidwell lived with the Mechoopda for three weeks when he first came to the area. He also ran a little trading post at the Patrick's Rancheria, south of Chico.

When the gold rush came, Bidwell hired about 20 Mechoopda from the Chico area to help him mine at Bidwell's Bar. The first Mechoopda village noted by John Bidwell was Chulamsewi, originally a summer camp. This had, perhaps, become a more permanent residence for the Mechoopda, because Bidwell found them there still when he purchased Rancho del Arroyo Chico from William Dickey. Before he made the land purchase, he had made several trips to the Mechoopda area for various reasons. His relationship with them, from the beginning, was affable.

Before the purchase of his land, Bidwell, still in the employ of John Sutter, who was an influential settler of the Sacramento area, performed a census of the Central Valley north of Sacramento in 1847. The survey revealed "82 whites, 19 tame Indians and 19,000 wild Indians." The caucasian population in 1848 was 82 persons. By 1850, it was 3,541 persons. This statement alone tells the impact of the gold rush on the communities in northern California. The population of Bidwell's Bar at the time was 600. The natives were not as affected by the first wave of settlers, who were generally local miners already settled with families. They were understanding of the rights of others. The second wave was made up of adventure seekers, opportunists, criminals, and runaways, who were not a considerate bunch.

The natives had lived in equilibrium with nature. That balance was now being upset by the influx of miners, with their dogs, cattle, horses, and other domestic animals. In the 60 years following 1850, this influx caused a massive faunal change that was matched only by the extinction of the postglacial period. Some species of condor, elk, grizzly bear, and antelope disappeared completely.

Another detrimental blow to the native population was the trading of their land for commodities by signing treaties. In 1851, treaties were made with the north Central Valley natives. They were signed at Bidwell's Ranch, at Colusa, and along the Yuba and Consumnes Rivers. The United States agreed to give the natives reservation land and some economic aid.

On August 1, 1851, the headmen of the tribes or villages of the Mechoopda, Eskuin, Hololupi, Toto, Sunus, Cheno, Batsi, Yutduc, and Simsawa were called together at Bidwell's Ranch to sign a treaty with Oscar M. Wozencraft, a U.S. Indian Agent. Each person 15 years of age or older was promised: 1 pair of pantaloons, 1 red flannel, 1 linsey gown for each woman or girl, 2,000 yards of calico, 500 yards of brown sheeting, 20 pounds of Scotch thread, 1,000 needles, six dozen thimbles, two dozen pairs of scissors, 1 two-and-a-half point Mackinaw blanket, 1,000 pounds of iron, 100 milch cows, 6 bulls, 4 yoke work cattle and chains, 6 work mules or horses, 12 ploughs of assorted sizes, 75 garden or corn hoes, 25 spades, and 4 grindstones.

Each of the headmen made their mark of agreement. Kulmeh, the leader of the Konkau tribe, would not sign. He wished to keep his village and did not believe the words of white men. This man was the great-grandfather of Henry Azbill, a native historian of the early 1900s.

Immediately after these documents were signed, the California Senate appointed a committee to research the area so that any gold-bearing, or valuable, land would not be given to the Indians as reservation land. They wanted to rid the state of Indians so the treaties did not have to be kept. One year later, in 1852, they rejected all the treaties without waiting for the state to be rid of the Indians, so anxious were they to mine the gold-bearing dirt of the state.

Between mining and agriculture, the California settlers took all the land they wanted from the natives, with little interference. Natives were killed, without fear of punishment, if a white settler deemed it to their benefit to do so.

When John Bidwell moved the Mechoopda village over to his side of the creek, very close to his adobe home in 1852, he placed himself downstream in a position that he thought would serve well to protect them. The name of this relocated Mechoopda village was Bahapki.

Mrs. Amanda Wilson was a long-time employee of the Bidwells and the widowed wife of both Holi Lafonso and Santa Wilson, the last of the chiefs on the Bidwell Rancheria. She recorded 32 songs on cylinders, for a gramophone, during her lifetime. She was from the Konkau Tribe. In 1946, she was about 100 years old.

When the Spaniards began to explore the Americas and Franciscan Fathers brought the missions to California, the Maidu way of life faced enormous adjustments. The changes almost destroyed the elaborate culture, food system, ceremonies, and territories the Maidu had sustained for a thousand years or more. Disease and displacement were the initial changes, then the gold rush and greed sealed the fate of the native people. The Spanish and Mexican land grants, ranching, gold mining, the lumber industry, the westward expansion of the United States, trade, and new ways of transportation all converged on California from 1840 to 1850, making sweeping and irreversible changes for the population in the state, but particularly in the Sacramento Valley because it was the center of gold commerce.

In the words of Rod Clements, present day council member for the Mechoopda Tribe:

> It was a time of profound social, cultural and political change. In just over a decade, the Mechoopda, and all Maidu people, went from open, autonomous village communities in and around present day Butte County, to secluded remnant pockets relegated to servitude to white landowners in order to maintain their survival and traditional lifestyles.

Chapter Three

PIONEERS AND GOLDMINES

John Bidwell was born in New York in 1819. He spent most of his childhood working on his father's farm. His father was from Connecticut, a farmer, not wealthy, and his mother, Clarissa Griggs, was from Massachusetts. He had limited schooling and was mostly self-taught. When he was 19, he decided to move west. First he went to the state of Ohio where he attended school at the Kingsville Academy. He writes, "The spring of 1839 in Ohio being in my twentieth year, I conceived a desire to see the plains of the great west. Starting on foot to Cincinnati, ninety miles distant, fortunately I got a ride most of the way on a farm wagon loaded with produce." Bidwell had $75, the clothes he was wearing, and a few others in a knapsack. He had only a pocketknife for a weapon. Rivers were the chief highways of travel at that time. Passengers that tried to ride a boat were charged for 150 pounds of freight as their ticket.

After his first term at the academy, he took the teacher's exam and spent the rest of his time there as a schoolmaster. Some accounts say he was the head schoolmaster. John Bidwell was both academic and adventurous, and despite his humble apologies as a writer and historian, left tremendous insight into the times and locations he visited through his letters, diaries, notes, and accounting records.

After two years in Ohio, he moved west to Missouri, presumably to obtain adventure and land. He claimed a plot on the west side of the Missouri River where he settled on 160 acres. After building a fence and doing some improvements, he left for St. Louis, Missouri, to get some supplies. While he was gone, a claim jumper built a cabin on his land.

The parcel Bidwell lost was on a tract of land in Platte County, Missouri. It was fertile black soil with clear water springs, rolling hills, and had a peaceful feeling. When he claimed the land, he had spent his money in travels, so he began teaching school. Bidwell lost this claim to a "scoundrel" who had killed a man in Calloway County, or so it was rumored. He gave up hope of regaining his claim and turned his attention to another place he had heard of—California. He met Roubideaux, a French man who had been to California. Bidwell says, "His description of the country made it sound like paradise."

John Bidwell was interested in stories about the land west of the Rocky Mountains. He was determined to go and discover it for himself. He stayed to finish teaching at the school the winter of 1840, but planned to move on. In the spring of 1841, John joined a group called the "Western Emigration Society." Five hundred people had joined, but when it came time to leave in May of 1841, only John Bidwell and one other wagon of travelers were prepared to go. They waited several more days and finally rounded up a total of 69 travelers. The group included Bartleson, a self-proclaimed leader, and his eight men, a convention of six Jesuit priests, a fur-trader named Thomas "Broken Hand" Fitzpatrick (who was useful in dealing with all the native tribes they met), a woman, and a child.

Since there were less than 100 Americans living in all of California at the time, there were no maps describing how to get there. John Bidwell left Missouri, a 21-year-old man, with this group of adventurers. The party did not travel together the whole journey. They split into three groups after leaving Soda Springs, on the other side of the Continental Divide. A few of the original 69 persons turned back, and one unfortunate individual accidentally shot himself and died. Bidwell's portion of the group later became known as the Bidwell-Bartelson Party. There were 34 people involved, including 32 men, one woman, and one child. They lost Thomas Fitzpatrick's help when he went to Oregon with some of the travelers, and the Jesuit priests joined with a group of Flathead Indians and left to establish a mission near Missoula, Montana.

The journey from that point for the Bidwell-Bartelson Party was largely uncharted. Bidwell himself said, "Our ignorance of the route was complete." John Bidwell was a young man and not the leader of the group, although he did become known as the scout and pathfinder. His party had to abandon their wagons after leaving Salt Lake and went on with oxen, packsaddles, horses, and mules. The Hudson Bay Company warned them that they couldn't go too far south, or they would die in deserts, and they couldn't go too far north, or they would get caught in snowdrifts.

The road was arduous without the wagons, and when the party got to the Sierras, they were overwhelmed by the vast tracklessness of the great expanse of mountains. Bidwell describes them as "veritable terra incognita." His journal on October 18 of the year he crossed the Sierras states, "A frightful prospect opened before us, naked mountains, whose summits still retained the snows, perhaps of a thousand years. The wind roared, but in the deep, dark gulfs which yawned on every side, profound solitude seemed to reign."

In the throes of this disillusionment, Bartleson, the famed leader of the assembly, and his eight followers took off alone and left the remainder of the group, including the woman and a child, to cross the immense mountain range without his help or that of his men. They took a supply of meat and abandoned the others in the treacherous maze of the Sierras in the fall of 1841. Bidwell stayed with the main group. The deserters eventually ran out of food and had less success negotiating the crossing of the Sierras than Bidwell's group. The two halves eventually rejoined. They had taken their packsaddles, animals, horses, oxen, and mules. Supplies ran low and food was scarce as they crossed the Sierras, thus the oxen were consumed as food before the trip was over.

After many adversities, the Bidwell-Bartelson party made it across the Sierra Nevadas on October 31, fortunately before new snow started to fall. Their first real meal in many days was a coyote. Two days after this feast, and surely after many thoughts of perishing, they crossed the mountains and a huge valley stretched in front of them. They descended the western slope of a range along Stanislaus River into the San Joaquin Valley. Bidwell and his group thought they had to cross the valley and then go over another mountain range before they came to California. After days of walking and riding, and a hostile encounter with Native Americans just as they left the mountains, they came to Mount Diablo and met a Dr. Marsh who lived there. At Marsh's Ranch they were overjoyed to learn that they were in California. They were one of the first groups of white settlers to cross the Sierra Nevada range, the other party being the Bonneville group in 1833, nearly ten years previously.

A joy, equaling Bidwell's previous despair, was recorded at the crossing of the Sierra Crest. The party had encountered a wild maze of ridges and canyons, through which they wandered for more than a week when Bidwell wrote:

> We had gone about three miles when lo! To our great delight we beheld a wide valley!
> Rivers evidently meandered through it, for timber seen in long lines as far as the eye could

reach. Saw many tracks of elk. Wild fowls were flying in multitudes . . . joyful sight to us poor famished wretches! I met many Indians, or rather several villages of Indians. They made no attempt to interfere with me.

When the immigrants arrived in central California, they found a landscape of almost unimaginable natural bounty . . . yet one which, within a generation, would largely disappear. John Bidwell's early writings provide us with a vivid picture of this pristine world in its twilight:

> I would like to give you an idea of the general character and features of this country . . . the great central feature, if I may use the term, is this Grand Valley of the Sacramento and San Joaquin. It is bounded on the East by the Sierra Nevada Mountains, famous for their abundant snows. When the snows melt, the waters converge into mighty rivers, overflowing their banks, covering the plains like an inland sea. Tule marshes occupy large portions of the valley. These are the haunts of incalculable thousands of wild geese, ducks, cranes, pelicans. . . . For miles you might travel in early spring and beautiful flowers fairly paint the landscape in their rich profusion. Broad prairies covered with wild oats would be along your road. . . . The valley was, apparently, still as new as when Columbus discovered America, and abounded in elk, deer, antelope, beaver, and otter. Grizzly bear were almost an hourly sight.

Just as the natural setting proved an endless source of wonder to an easterner, so also did the cultural scene. The "Alta California" of those days was a remote, sparsely populated Mexican province that only 20 years earlier had won its independence from Spain. Bidwell found:

> . . . The White population confined to a narrow belt along the coast, extending from Russian River to San Diego. There are no large towns. Monterey is the principal, and contains about 500 inhabitants. Missions are nearly all broken up, and those that remain are fast declining. One Spanish league, about 6 1/2 square miles, is considered a farm. . . . At this time there was not in California any vehicle except a rude cart, drawn by oxen. There was not to my knowledge a lawyer or law-book, post office or mail route, printing office or newspaper; nor was there any military force to speak of. General Vallego was Commander-in-Chief, and lived at Sonoma. He kept there about thirty soldiers. Little inspiration was needed to feel that government so feebly equipped could not long endure.

After obtaining a passport at mission San Jose, Bidwell returned to the interior, having heard that a man named John Sutter was starting a colony there. Dr. Marsh told John Bidwell about John Sutter, a German with a large ranch and many enterprises near what is now the city of Sacramento. After a few days' adventure, including being locked up in jail when trying to obtain a passport, Bidwell and several companions, finally freed and carrying passports, rode to see Sutter. Bidwell and Sutter, who was a magnanimous man with vision, got along very well. Bidwell was hired and began a long relationship of friendship and employment with the man. Bidwell served as Sutter's "factorum" secretary, ranch manager, project manager for various projects, and aide-de-camp during military expeditions.

Pioneers and Goldmines

It was a young territory with only 7,000 non-Indian residents in the entire state; most of these were citizens of Mexico and were almost all living on the coast. There were not many more than 100 Americans. Johan Augustus Sutter was a man of German-Swiss heritage who had immigrated to the United States in 1834. He had decided to come west to establish a business, and had first gone to Hawaii in search of supplies and returned to the west coat of California with materials and a crew of Hawaiians. He obtained a large land grant in the Sacramento Valley. Sutter's grant was 11 square leagues and extended through the valley nearly as far north as Marysville. He staffed it with Americans, Hawaiians, and Indians. This may have provided Bidwell a model for establishing his own ranch eight years later.

John Sutter viewed Bidwell as a capable man, a "strong right arm." Bidwell's first assignment was to catalog and deliver supplies purchased from the Russians, who were leaving Fort Ross on the Northern California coast. Subsequent assignments included surveying, mapping, and establishing documentation for claimants of land grants to the north of Sutter's property.

His first journey into the Chico area was with Peter Lassen, a Danish immigrant who, according to his nephew, wrote a history of Lassen's adventures, was magnanimous and capable and loved to help others get ventures going. The trip Lassen and Bidwell made to the Chico Creek area was in March 1843. While still in Sutter's employ, Bidwell and Lassen joined up with James Bruheim in 1843 to follow horse thieves and recover them. Bidwell was struck by the beauty of the Chico Creek area and he returned on another journey to make maps of the area. He learned that the land grants ended just north of the Chico Creek. This excerpt from Bidwell's writing explains what he thought about the land surrounding the creek:

> Hastening up the valley, we struck the trail of the Oregon Company on what is now known as Chico Creek, Rancho Chico, and to me one of the loveliest of places. The plains were covered with scattered groves of spreading oaks; there were wild grasses and clover, two, three and four feet high, and most luxuriant. The fertility of the soil was beyond question, and the waters of Chico Creek were clear, cold and sparkling; the mountains were lovely and flower-covered, a beautiful scene. In a word, this chase was the means of locating me for life. I never was permanently located till I afterward located here. It was early in March, 1843, when we reached Chico Creek.

By spring of 1846, Bidwell had helped 21 settlers find places and apply for land grants in the Sacramento Valley area. It was about this time that he started to go through the process necessary to become a Mexican citizen and obtain a land grant of his own. In 1844, he received title to the Ulpinos land grant in the Sacramento Delta area, but he never settled on this property. Bidwell actually took up residence on the Little Butte Creek, at the Farwell Grant. He and Edward Farwell were partners, perhaps in the ownership of cattle and horses, but to what extent is not recorded.

Dickey and Farwell beat Bidwell to Chico. Bidwell would buy land from these gentlemen that would eventually become the site of the city of Chico. In 1842, Farwell arrived in Monterrey, California from Boston for health reasons. At the time of his arrival in California, cowhides were known as "the California Bank Note" and went for $2 apiece. He met William Dickey, an Irishman, in Monterrey, and together they decided to make a living raising cattle to obtain their share of cowhides. The polished young Micheltorena, the Mexican governor, was generous with Americans.

CHICO

Dickey and Farwell had heard of the Sutter settlement in New Helvetia on the Sacramento River. Sutter had been made the military magistrate for Northern California, and Governor Micheltorena was approving Sutter's recommendations for land grants.

Farwell and Dickey traveled by launch up the Sacramento River to Sutter's home. They were received cordially, and Sutter encouraged them to become land ranchers. Applications for land grants had been made east of the Feather River, and as far north as Little Butte Creek above the Sutter Buttes.

Settlers had obtained land from Sutter's outpost, New Helvetica, to the Chico Creek. Nicholas Altgier's ranch was on the Feather River east of Hock Farm, Sebastian Keyser's was on the north bank of the Bear River, and the Frenchmen, Channon and Sicard, were on the south bank. William Nye was on Yuba River, and Theodore Cordula had settled on Feather River and had established a trading post for Sutter. Charles Roether had decided to locate on Honcut Creek, and Thomas Fallon was nearby. Samuel Neal had chosen Butte Creek, and William Northgraves, Little Butte Creek. Sutter encouraged Farwell and Dickey to travel north of the Northgraves ranch and take a look. He loaned them horses and provisions.

Dickey and Farwell equipped themselves with guns and ammunition, and an Indian guide led them as far as Cordula's trading post. They stayed overnight, and the next day they traveled on and came to a much smaller creek than others they had seen where they made camp. It was Chico Creek. Fish could be caught in all seasons, the game was good, the climate nice; it was peaceful, and they liked it.

They decided on two 5-league parcels north and south of Chico Creek, which was just east of the Sacramento River. A league was 1,500 Roman paces, or 1.37 English miles. The pair flipped to see who would get north and who south. Farwell won and got the south. They returned to Sutter's Fort and applied for the grants. By then it was 1843. The following March, John Bidwell came through the area. He went as far north as Red Bluff in search of stolen horses.

In 1845, Manuel Micheltorena, serving under the famous president of Mexico, General Antonio Santa Anna, hoped to see the Americans help him settle the land and make it a prosperous place. Californians of Spanish decent resented both Mexicans and Americans. Spaniards and other discontents began a rebellion against Santa Anna, his Governor Micheltorena, and their friendly attitude toward the Americans. Juan Bautista Alvarado and Jose Castro were the organizers. Their following was largely in the southern part of the state. When news of Alvarado and Castro's rebellion spread, Sutter went with Micheltorena, as did John Bidwell (Sutter's aide de camp). Alvarado and Castro were chased to Los Angeles by 80 American riflemen, including Sutter and Bidwell. The Spaniards surprised Sutter and the Mexicans at the Cahuenga Pass outside of Los Angeles. The American riflemen did not shoot. Sutter and Micheltorena were captured, but since there was no shooting, they were released again. California wine flowed freely that evening. Governor Micheltorena was sent back to Mexico City, and Sutter went home to Sacramento. Castro and Alvarado prevailed, but only for one year.

In December, Captain John C. Fremont of the army appeared at Sutter's Fort, where Bidwell tried to accommodate him and his 60 armed men. Since there was not an uprising at the time, Fremont's troop was supposedly on a mission of exploration; however, Fremont did some posturing with the Mexican government. On his way to Monterrey from Sutter's Fort, he was ordered by Castro to steer clear of California's settlements. Instead, he and his troops climbed to the top of Gavilan Peak, raised the American flag for all to see, and stayed for five days before departing for Oregon. When

Fremont returned to the Sutter Buttes in May, many Americans in California talked of setting the territory free from Mexican rule.

The Bear Flag Revolt reportedly emanated from Fremont and his camp at the base of the Sutter Buttes, although in reality many of the participants were largely acting on their own. William B. Ide was instrumental in the revolt. He had an adobe home on the Sacramento River at the site of the Adobe Ferry. His ranch was Rancho De Barranca Colorado (Red Bluff Ranch). Peter Lassen, owner of the Lassen land grant to the north, joined, as did Ezekiel Merritt and Kit Carson's brother, Moses.

The story is that Ide and Merritt captured a band of Mexican soldiers and confiscated 200 horses. They deposited these horses at Fremont's camp at the Sutter Buttes, and then, taking a band of rebels, left for Sonoma, where the Bear Flag Revolt began in earnest. Ide and his 20 followers forcibly took the settlement of Sonoma from Mexico, raising the Bear Flag on June 14, 1846.

They captured General Mariano Vallejo in Sonoma. He was brought to Bidwell at Sutter's Fort and placed under Bidwell's supervision. Bidwell gladly gave up the job of supervising the Mexican general to Fremont's lieutenant. He then left for Sonoma to join the other Bears. The united forces of Fremont and the Bears marched on Monterrey in July. The independent California Republic was only in existence for 26 days before the federal government took up the cause and declared war on Mexico. Ide was the first and only president of the Republic of California during its 26-day existence. Bidwell was inextricably involved in this conflict from 1846, when he left to join Ide in Sonoma, until January of 1847, when Fremont received the surrender of Alvarado and Castro at the notorious Cahuenga Pass, north of Los Angeles. This is where Sutter and Bidwell had been temporarily taken prisoner two years previously. Bidwell embroiled in the conflict, and ever the writer, drafted what has been called the briefest constitution on record: "The undersigned hereby agree to organize for the purpose of gaining and maintaining the independence of California."

Twice during this war, Bidwell had saved his own life by taking refuge on a federal ship in the harbor. He was appointed the "alcalde" of the Mission San Luis Rey in Los Angeles during the conflict, and later the chief magistrate of Orange and San Diego Counties in California.

Bidwell served in a group of Californians who held the Constitutional Convention in Monterrey in 1849. He represented the Sacramento District (all of northern California) in the first state legislature. He took a block of gold-bearing quartz to Washington, D.C. to commemorate George Washington's birthday and helped convince secretary of state to admit California into the Union. Upon returning, he was able to announce that statehood was accomplished. California was admitted to the Union on September 9 of 1850. It was the 31st state.

At the end of the Mexican War, Bidwell remained in Sutter's employ for over a year, although he wanted to go back to Rancho Chico to Farwell's property and farm. In December of 1847, Sutter and the new governor of California, Richard Mason, assigned Bidwell to conduct a census survey of the California Indians. Bidwell's assignment encompassed the northern Sacramento Valley, north of the Sutter Buttes. Some groups of Indians defied census, like the Kombo tribes, which were roving communities that lived in caves and temporary camps along Mill and Deer Creeks.

A group of so-called "Indian Fighters" formed in the Chico area. Hi Goode, Bob Anderson, Sam Carey, William McIntyre, William Lindsay, Tom and Jim Roger, Hank Smith, Jack Houser, Tom Gore, Bolivar McGee, "Bully" Bowman, and Henry Curtis were self-proclaimed Indian Fighters and eventually became known in the community.

CHICO

During the Mexican War, the California natives had not fared well. A military order of 1847 and State Legislative Act of 1850 allowed any unemployed Indian to be declared a vagrant and forced to work on public lands, or to be auctioned off as indentured servants. It was a common practice to kidnap natives, especially children, to be sold as household or farm servants.

Unknown to Bidwell at the time, far greater changes were coming. He was still an employee of John Sutter, and his assignment to take a census of the northern Sacramento Valley gave him an opportunity to return with cattle to Farwell's ranch. While there he built his first cabin, which was located on Little Butte Creek. It was made of oak and sycamore logs chinked with mud. The opening was covered with deerskins. Inside were two bunks with a window over each bunk, covered with cloth. It was a primitive start for Bidwell.

His next project for Sutter was the construction of a sawmill in the Sierra foothills, at the Maidu village of Coloma, on the south fork of the American River. This project was destined to become Bidwell's fortune, and although no one knew it at the time, it was also Chico's fortune, and the fortune of thousands who would inundate the state of California. According to Bidwell, "Sutter's wants for lumber increased year by year, and it became his custom to send men into the mountains to search for a place to build a sawmill. In 1846 he sent me. In 1847 he happened to send Marshall."

The location Marshall chose was in a remote, steep-walled valley about 45 miles from Sutter's Fort. Bidwell's description continues:

> Marshall was a very curious fellow. It is hard to conceive how any sane man could have selected such a site for a sawmill. Surely no other man than Marshall ever entertained so wild a scheme as that of rafting sawed lumber down the canyons of the American River, and no other man than Sutter would have been so confiding and credulous as to patronize him. Yet the two together by this means, turned the world upside down.

In January 1848, some flecks of gold caught the eye of carpenter James Marshall. Bidwell reports:

> It was the beginning of a new epoch, from all states and countries thousands rushed into California. Sacramento City was laid off on the river two miles west of the fort and the town grew up there at once into a city. It became the bustling, buzzing center for merchants, traders, miners, etc., and every available room was in demand. Here were brought into contrast scenes of order, good will and noblest friendship, against anarchy, outrage and crime.

Gold was discovered at the mill site while digging the tailrace for the building. Bidwell was in on the discovery, and the three men—Sutter, Marshall, and Bidwell—were to keep it secret, but by May of the same year the gold rush of California was on. By autumn, reports were circulating in the East, and by 1849, the entire world knew. No one knows who let the news out, but Bidwell does mention in journal entries that Sutter could not keep a secret.

Bidwell began prospecting in earnest by April that year with native help. Bidwell did not pay the natives with money at first. In fact, it was hard to get the local natives to work for money. They wanted goods, and previous to the gold rush, the exchange in California was largely accomplished with commodities. However, the low value of goods traded with the native people for their labor was unfair. Bidwell records in his early days at Bidwell's Bar, "I had brought five or six Indians with me. They soon learned that there was value in the gold, and gave up cheerfully all they had for sugar."

Bidwell's Bar was located on the middle fork of the Feather River, northeast of Oroville, and not far from Chico. He arrived with four of the neighbors from the Farwell Ranch. Discouraged with their results, two of the men left first and, then eventually, they all went home. Later, from his cabin on the Farwell property in 1848, Bidwell assembled a larger company of Indians and returned to mine at Bidwell's Bar.

Bidwell came back with Northgraves, one of the neighbors that had stuck with him, and a crew of 20 Indian workers. Bidwell finally took leave of Sutter's employment, heading for Rancho Chico, his cattle, and Bidwell's Bar to prospect gold. He also found success with supplying gold miners from a store he set up at Bidwell's Bar. He easily could have accumulated more gold by trading supplies to the miners than by panning gold for himself. At any rate, he became rich with his ventures at Bidwell's Bar and quickly converted his riches for land and supplies to farm.

Mining was rough business and Bidwell was well read, a writer, a businessman, and an adventurer. Not lacking in courage or moral fortitude, the trade end of the mining business would certainly have appealed to him more than staking a claim, which he never did. Mine claims often ended in disputes, shootings or knifings, and even death. It was rumored that Bidwell had only mediocre success in gold panning, and possibly the money he made was from the store he opened. Many entrepreneurs traded goods to the miners at inflated prices. Despite amplified prices for expenses, many of the miners got rich. One might pay $150 to rent a rocker for a day. A barrel of flour might cost $800. At any rate, Bidwell retired from mining ventures with roughly $100,000 worth of gold.

Many worthless, and even criminal, men were miners. They ate bad food, bacon, flapjacks, and coffee, often in unrecognizable forms. They made up ballads, sang, fiddled, and played banjo. They also fought and stole claims from each other and took revenge. It was a wild and lawless time.

Bidwell was one to do things officially and had worked at documenting his career. He established the town of Bidwell's Bar on July 4, 1848. During the fever of the gold rush it became the county seat of Butte County for a short period, but it was always a busy trading center and mining camp. The first fluming of the rivers was done at Bidwell's Bar, and the first newspaper in the area, the *Butte Record*, was published from there as well.

By fall of 1853, Bidwell's Bar had a population of 1,800 people. The town was almost destroyed in a fire in 1854, but it was quickly rebuilt. The famous suspension bridge was built there and later moved to higher ground. Actually completed in 1855, the first traffic crossed the suspension bridge in 1856. The night of the opening, a big celebration was held, and the dance lasted from evening until dawn. Guns were collected at the entrance and returned as people went home. By 1856, the gold-bearing sands were exhausted. Bidwell's Bar became a deserted village, but it once had three general stores and a saloon with a theatre. John Bidwell had set aside property for a plaza where community gatherings were held. When new diggings opened in Ophir (now Oroville) in 1855–1856, most of Bidwell's Bar's citizens moved there.

In 1856, oranges from Mazatlan were planted in the Sacramento Valley. Judge Joseph, of Bidwell's Bar, purchased a two-year-old Mazatlan orange tree of this variety. In 1923, that tree measured 31 feet, 6 inches tall. The average spread of branches was 30 feet in circumference, a foot above the ground. It was said to have turned the gold in the ground to gold in the trees, especially as more people planted and cared for its seedlings. This tree was termed the "Mother Orange."

The Oroville Dam was constructed roughly 100 years later, and the bust mining town founded by John Bidwell, seven years before he laid out the city of Chico, went underwater. Before the dam waters covered the town site, the suspension bridge was preserved by moving it to higher ground, and the "Mother Orange" tree was transplanted at the same time.

The gold rush began with self-employed, gold-panning miners in 1848–1849. The trend quickly changed to larger groups, working rockers, and sluice boxes in the 1850s. By 1852, corporate-owned mines employed miners for wages. Ditches, flumes, and high-pressure hydraulic mining appeared shortly after.

The miners polluted the environment with "slickens," the debris from the mining processes that filled the rivers and caused further flooding damage as a side effect. The mining efforts destroyed fish habitats and played havoc with navigation routes on the rivers, running through the valley that had been established earlier. The bed of the Yuba River was raised 30 feet by mining debris.

Mining deposited silt and debris into creeks and rivers, causing havoc during winter. During the Great Flood of 1862, between December 1, 1861, and the end of January 1862, over 23 inches of rain fell in the area. Fifteen of those inches fell in January. By the end of the month, the city of Sacramento was inundated. Chinatown in Oroville was entirely sluiced out. Adobe buildings "melted" and disappeared. Many took refuge in the Sutter Buttes, and many cattle died.

The floods and silt deposits from the mining continued to cause problems; levees broke, property was destroyed, and farmers were unhappy with the miners. In 1870, a horticulture and fruit farming association was formed. Injunctions, restrictions, resolutions, and restraints were put on hydraulic mining. The Caminetti Act set up the Anti-Debris Commission in the state. At the end of the hydraulic mining period, enterprises began dredging the Feather River for more gold.

Dredging for gold was profitable from 1898 to 1918. Nearly $30 million in gold was extracted in the Oroville area, making Butte County the top spot for gold mining. However, it left ugly mounds of gravel and muddied the waters of the Feather River.

In reality, despite the lobbying of the farming groups, including the Anti-Debris Commission started by John Bidwell, their plight was fairly ineffective. The gold mining and polluting activities of the industry did not stop until the gold became scarce and it was no longer profitable for companies to mine.

Bidwell formed the State Agricultural Society and lobbied against mining. Finally, long after it would have been most effective, a judgment in the case of Edwards Woodruff in 1884 helped somewhat to put a stop to mining pollution. Woodruff was the owner of a farm on the Feather River near Marysville who sued the North Bloomfield Mining Company for damage done to his property by mining debris. Judge Lorenzo Sawyer ruled the Northern Bloomfield Mining Company a nuisance.

Bidwell turned from mining to farming and employed both Chinese and natives on his ranch, and even though threatened by the populace in general, stood for their rights and guaranteed their jobs. At the time, this was a very unpopular stance.

The Chinese came to California in the 1850s and 1860s in a time when chaos and domination by outside forces ruled China. Many Chinese fled. Some joined the rush to find gold in California. The Chinese that came to Butte County were from Guangzhou, the capital of Guan don (Canton).

Originally, the Chinese worked claims already exhausted by white men. Their style of mining was called "coyote mining." A well would be dug several feet deep. The dirt was put in buckets and hauled to the top, and then put in sluice boxes to wash out the gold. Chinese were "coyote mining" near Ophir, later named Oroville, in 1856, and in the Lava Beds on the riverbanks where digging was easier.

The Chinese built a town southwest of Oroville on the Feather River. It was called Bagdad. They planted gardens with nutmeg and lemon trees and fields of mint. They were frugal and stuck together, not mixing with whites. They retained their language, food, and dress style. In 1860, there were 2,177 Chinese in Butte County. In the early 1870s, there were an estimated 10,000 Chinese living in the Oroville area.

Rock walls were built around Chico between 1860 and 1890 with lava rock gathered from the land. The crews that performed this work included Chinese, some Irish, and others. Lish Richardson, part owner of the Richardson Springs resort outside of Chico, was among the first to start building the walls. A crew of laborers cleared the land of volcanic rock and created fences at the same time.

By 1860, Chinese were 15 percent of the population in Butte County. There were several Chinatowns in Chico. The first was on Flume Street, extending to Orient Street, between Fifth and Sixth Streets. Two-story wooden buildings were constructed with shops on the first floor and living quarters on the second story. The buildings had wooden porches and plank sidewalks. The merchants would display their wares on the sidewalk, protected from sun and weather by the porch roof. Elderly Chinese men would sit near the goods watching them and visiting with each other. Below the east side of Flume Street, a labyrinth basement ran the whole length of the block. This is probably what gave rise to all the rumors in Chico about the Chinese having secret underground tunnels. Two tunnels from downtown hotels ran underground to the Chinese red light district, which was along Wall Street. Some interconnecting of basements have been found, but the legendary labyrinth, or secret system of tunnels, made by the Chinese was more imaginary than real.

Most of the business in Old Chinatown was conducted in one large block. The community had an unofficially appointed mayor, a friendly, outgoing person named Ching Hi. During the peak years of Chinatown, many people from Chico ate in the Chinese restaurants and shopped in the stores. Lew Ed was the first man to open a Chinese import store in town. Its inauguration was in 1900, and he maintained business there for 30 years. Huie Pock, an herb doctor, was also popular in town. His store was on the corner of Sixth and Flume. Doctor Oscar Stansbury, a prominent Chico citizen, described the Chinese as "fine, self-reliant and uncomplaining people." After a visit to Chinatown he wrote this description:

> Dinner over, we strolled along the narrow dingy streets of Chinatown, its houses squalid and huddled together. Still at night there was an exotic quality about it. Bright flashes of color relieved the gloomy and rather sinister surroundings. Large, pot-bellied lanterns with red lettering swung from the balconies. Yellow and vermilion strips of crepe paper bearing strange characters hung from windows. Beautiful, green pottery and bright silks were displayed in shop windows. With all this there was a mingling of odors, of musk and incense, of fish and vegetables, of tobacco and burning punk. The streets were crowded with blue-bloused Chinese who shuffled past, silent and indifferent.

Later, around 1869, a new Chinatown grew on Cherry Street between Seventh and Ninth Streets, with a temple on the corner of West Eighth and Cherry. The area was different from Old Chinatown as many of the buildings were one story. They were set back off the road, and the front of the lots were planted in gardens. The plots were beautiful and useful, containing mostly vegetables. A Joss house, or Chinese place of worship, was built on the corner of Eighth and Cherry Streets. New Chinatown burned in 1873 and had to be built again, almost from scratch. After the fire, the *Chico Record* demonstrated a clearly prejudiced and unsympathetic attitude toward the Chinese, stating, "It is a pity that these Chinese nuisances have to be put up with. . . . these people must live somewhere, and it is better that they should be together and alone." Meaning, separate from the rest of the populace.

A third Chinatown was built on Humboldt Road, along the banks of the Little Chico Creek. The Sierra Lumber Company employed most of the residents of this neighborhood. This was not a commercial Chinatown like the others, but the families did keep animals in their basements and in cages inside their homes, probably raising them for sale, or possibly for their own consumption. Fire destroyed this Chinatown also, and neighbors were reportedly slow to call the volunteer fire department. This settlement was never rebuilt. The families from the Humboldt Road Chinatown were assimilated into the two other Chinatowns in Chico.

In the later 1870s, a stronger wave of anti-Chinese sentiment grew in Chico. The *Butte County Free Press*, first issued in Chico, later became the *Chico Caucasian* because of anti-Chinese sentiment. In 1882, the first Chinese Exclusion Act was passed, suspending the immigration of Chinese to the United States. As anti-Chinese sentiment grew, the Chinese left. As the Chinese left, people began hiring Japanese to pick fruit in the Gridley and Chico areas. In 1894, another Anti-Chinese League formed in Chico to petition that farmers hire only white labor.

Chinese were murdered in their cabins, and their belongings were taken. Dr. Oscar Stansbury of Chico tells of an event that occurred before his fiancée, Libbie, joined him on the western frontier in 1877:

> The white folks were out of work and anti-Chinese feelings grew . . . group of drunk white men went out to the Lemm Ranch, where a crew of Chinese were working, and robbed the Chinese and then gunned them down and killed six people in cold blood.

This incident happened on January 27, 1877. Many people in town did not favor this type of action, even though they weren't sympathetic toward the Chinese. A search began for the perpetrators. They were thought to be from a group called the Order of the Caucasians or from the Labor Union that had formed. These groups included many prominent Chico area leaders in their membership.

The Labor Union was an anti-Chinese group formed out of discontent regarding the employment of the Chinese over caucasian workers at a time of economic stress. Chinese were willing to work for less, although they often worked as domestic help or were hired in Chinese businesses, positions that weren't sought by white workers. They did, however, do farm labor white workers were willing to do, which is where the contention began. Many white citizens in town were of the opinion that the Chinese were taking jobs from them because they worked hard and expected less pay. The newspaper urged a boycott of any and all persons favorable to Chinese.

Other groups organized around the same issue. A group called The Committee of One Hundred formed to counteract the Order of the Caucasians. These 100 citizens of Chico, some prominent leaders, included John Bidwell. They were disturbed about boycotting and otherwise persecuting innocent people who were not breaking the law. They supported the halt of Chinese immigration to the area, but wanted those that were already part of the community to be treated fairly. They ferreted out the ringleaders of the Order of the Caucasians.

An anonymous person mailed threatening letters to John Bidwell because he employed a number of Chinese workers on his ranch. Although seasonal employment for the Chinese had ended, Bidwell kept the workers on, so as not to let the "Caucasians think he had succumbed to their threats."

Bidwell stationed a man in the post office to discover who was posting the threatening letters. Eventually his sleuthing led to a person, Fred Conway, who had organized the Council of Nine. This group considered themselves an arm of the local Labor Union. Fred, four other adult men, and one boy were found guilty of the Lemm ranch crimes, which included robbery, murder in cold blood, and the burning of bodies and the quarters of the Chinese workers after their deaths. Two of the six Chinese men actually lived through this ordeal, and one had made it out of the burning building and reached the ranch owner that night to tell the story. With witnesses, the grand jury indicted and sentenced the men.

The Chinese were responsible for many individual, family, and community gardens around Chico. They also introduced Chinese varieties of fruits, trees, and flowers in the area. China Garden and China Camp Road in the Butte Creek Canyon area are named for their contributions. The Chinese in Butte County assisted in building the railroads. They helped build the community, but as crimes and sentiment against them grew more extreme, many left for larger cities or returned to China. Few families remained in Chico.

Dr. Stansbury hired a Chinese cook and a stableman who stayed in rough quarters. Of the Chinese cooks he said, "We could not do without them." And yet gradually most left Chico and people did have to do without them. Many Chinese went to larger colonies in Sacramento and San Francisco and Chico's Chinatowns gradually became deserted. Stansbury says:

> Looking back I think what a loss that has been to this town. Their color-ful parades on the Chinese New Year complete with a block-long dragon and exploding firecrackers with marchers dressed in their finest silks and satins; their funerals conducted with pomp and dignity and the sounds of flutes and gongs to drive away evil spirits; their joss houses where they worshipped their own god in their own way and, yes, the just plain dignity, industry and self reliance of those Chinese brought to this plain little valley town an exotic touch, an exposure to a way of life so foreign, yet so admirable, an Oriental charm that leaves us poorer with their going.

Chapter Four

RANCHO CHICO

With the proceeds from his mining ventures, John Bidwell purchased a portion of Rancho Chico from William Dickey on the north bank of the Big Chico Creek. Bidwell erected a long house there in the summer of 1849. In those years, raising stock was the principal industry outside mining. Bidwell, along with others, raised cattle for hides and tallow.

Bidwell eventually purchased all of William Dickey's 22,214 acres north of the creek and 4,000 acres from Edward E. Farwell just south of Big Chico Creek, which became Rancho Chico. The purchase seemed to have begun before the gold rush and ended after Bidwell struck it rich at Bidwell's Bar. He established a trading post and his home on Rancho Chico. In 1847, he managed experimental orchards and fields, flourmills, and fruit drying operations. This was just the beginning of Rancho Chico, which became a large enterprise during Bidwell's lifetime. He cared for the Mechoopda, on his land, in his own way. He taught them agriculture, offered free home sites, and paid them as laborers.

Bidwell had a model in mind of how to organize a ranch and use native labor, providing for their needs of shelter, employment, and education. No matter how John Bidwell tried to promote this plan, others did not catch on. It allowed him some high bumper crops of wheat and fruit, but others were not willing to try it. Perhaps because Bidwell had established such excellent rapport with most of the Mechoopda and was willing to take risks to employ them, it worked for him. The rest of the settlers in the state wanted to be rid of the "Indian problem." Dorothy Hill claims John Bidwell paid Indian laborers equal to white laborers, so the premise of retaining an inexpensive labor force, as it has been rumored that Bidwell's motive may have been, might not have been true.

Land was not worth much in the 1840s. No one knew how the territorial disputes and wars would resolve and if the claims would stick. The land was filling up with settlers. The northern border of Rancho Chico was 2.5 miles north of Chico Creek. Peter Lassen's land grant's southern border was 2.5 miles south of Deer Creek. Considerable territory lay between the two grants and many settlers squatted there. This was the case on all sides of the land grants.

Among the residents of early Chico in the 1840s and 1850s were: Randal Rice, Squire Wheeler, A.H. Barber, Dr. Luckett, Duncan Neal, Esquire Wright, Mr. McCutcheon, Mr. Chaney, John Potter, Uncle Johnny Whitesides, Solomon Gore, J.L. Keefer, the Wookey family, Bud Levens, Charley Pond, Joe Houghton, Thompson, Plez Guynn, Zach and D.F. Crowder, John and Nate Shannon, M.C. Sessions, Wes and Ike Bennett, J.W.B. Montgomery, Josh Broyles, Sam Bragg, the Daughtery family, the Hosler family, J.B. Clark, the Van Woerts, John Leininger, W.W. Davis, W.M. Thorpe, J.J. Waste, Mike Barnes, Coon Garner, John Helpenstein, Mr. Carmack, Redmond Richardson, and his two brothers, Ike Speegle and Uncle Dacy Rowles, Tom Polk, and Edward Bryson. Samuel Neal (Esquon Land Grant) and David Dutton settled just south of Chico, along Butte Creek.

Rancho Chico

It wasn't until 1853 that the federal government set up a land claims office in San Francisco, which confirmed land grants made in 1844 and before. At that time, A.W. Von Schmidt made a survey of Rancho Chico and presented the commissioner of the land office in San Francisco a patent to Rancho Chico on April 4, 1860.

The cabin home Bidwell built burned in 1852 and was replaced by a tavern built on the new property he purchased. It contained a barroom, dining room, kitchen, and sleeping rooms on the second story. Old timers remember the two spreading fig trees in front of the building. Bidwell, at this time, was busy raising cattle and directing a crew of Indians to clear many acres in preparation for planting wheat. He built a two-story adobe building at the entrance to his estate in 1852, after the first home burned. His adobe served as a residence and house for entertaining travelers along the Shasta-Tehama road.

Bidwell was constantly improving Rancho Chico. He tried a number of experiments in horticulture. He had at least one specimen from each of 400 varieties of fruit trees on his ranch. His was the first ranch to produce grapes commercially in California, and he was among the pioneers of olive oil production. He grew wheat and other grains on his farm and won awards in Paris and New Orleans for them.

John Bidwell cooperated with the Mechoopda to work on the land. The settlers, in general, did not consider the Indians people, but the two-story adobe house on Rancho Chico, which stood as John Bidwell's home for 16 years, was also home to half a dozen Mechoopda, mostly women, who did domestic chores. Nopanny, the chief's daughter, was Bidwell's cook and housekeeper until Annie Bidwell arrived at the ranch. She probably had been in this position for many years. She thought herself to be "Mrs. Bidwell number one."

By the time Mrs. Annie Bidwell met Nopanny, in the mansion that John built prior to her arrival, she had the status of head housekeeper and was a trusted employee. According to her admission, she was the first Mrs. Bidwell. Although there are no other accounts of this, it could explain the loyalty of the Indians to John Bidwell, and even perhaps John Bidwell's lack of interest in marrying for so many years. He apparently enjoyed Nopanny's company and her cooking. She served as head housekeeper, even after Annie's arrival at the mansion, until she died. Annie was younger, and outlived her by many years. With credit to Annie's wisdom, and probably even greater credit to her charity, she treated Nopanny with respect.

This little-discussed aspect of John Bidwell's life sheds light on Bidwell's reticence in fighting with any Indians, and his uncharacteristic foray as an Indian fighter when Maidu from the hills attacked the Mechoopda. The Mountain Indians had ample grievances with white men, who had taken over their hunting grounds and occupied their travel ways for hunting, gathering, and trading. Bidwell's Indians, or so the Mechoopda came to be called, were attacked by mountain Maidu in 1850. In a rare act against Indians, in order to protect the Mechoopda on his ranch, who were his friends as well as employees, Bidwell and one employee, Michael Nye, tracked the enemy group to the ridge where Nye was killed by an arrow, and Bidwell had a narrow escape.

The loyalty of the Mechoopda could also be explained by Bidwell's treatment of the people, and the special relationships he formed with key liaisons to the rest of the tribe, such as his employee, Raphael. He helped Bidwell secure individuals from the Mechoopda tribe on the ranch during times of persecution by secretly feeding tribal members as they hid in caves. He had a desire to incorporate the Mechoopda into the new way of life in California, and certain members of the tribe appreciated this.

CHICO

While new immigrants to the area, such as the Chinese, were persecuted and discriminated against for their differences, the original occupants of the territory, the Native Americans, also struggled to survive in the midst of the population influx of the gold rush. The Indian Appropriation Act of 1852 created five military reservations for Indians in California, Utah, and New Mexico. This was not an encouraging sign for the natives. The Nome Lakee reservation was constructed in 1854 in Tehama, and Maidu were rounded up and sent there.

Manoah Pence, a neighbor of Bidwell's to the south, was in partnership with four men on property just southeast of Chico. Pence reluctantly let Indians stay on his property overnight and they ran off his livestock. Pence and his ranch hands went to look for them. A battle ensued, and the chief was shot in the hip. He swore he'd have Pence's scalp. In 1853, Pence was involved in the hanging of one Indian who had been threatening the Clark Ranch and took part in a battle with some natives near Dogtown (Magalia) in which white men surrounded and fired on Indians in a camp until 25 out of 30 of them had been killed. In the fall of 1853, the Indians took revenge by massacring a camp of Chinese. Pence was asked to help track down and kill these natives. The Indian Fighters took 30 whites and 30 Chinese with them into the hills near Chico. They came upon the Indians at a nearby creek. Forty Indians were killed by the "fighters" in this attack.

Incidents like these continued over the next decade until 1862 when there was a meeting at the forks of Butte Creek between Oroville and Chico to decide what to do about the Mill Creek (mountain) Indians. A band of 24 white men wanted to avenge the murder of a teamster and the three missing children of Mrs. Hickok, her daughters aged 13 and 16, who had been shot with arrows, and their little brother, who was tortured to death.

The band, led by Harmon "Hi" Goode, searched for the natives who had harmed the children. In the spring of 1863, five Indians were hanged for the deaths of the Hickok children, at Helltown, which was located on Butte Creek south of Chico and west of the Paradise-Magalia ridge. This fanned Indian hatred of the whites. They killed several people living near Pence and then kidnapped the Lewis children, 12 miles northwest of Oroville in Berry Canyon. The children were walking home from school and stopped to get a drink at the creek. The older boy, Jimmy, was shot while kneeling to drink, and the Indians who fled took a four-year-old boy and a nine-year-old girl hostage. The little boy was crying, and the next morning he was taken away from the camp and stoned to death. Thankful Lewis, a little nine-year-old girl, waited until dark when only one native was guarding her, to make her escape. She hid behind a rock and struck out on her own, toward the nearest ranch. When the Indians discovered her missing, they backtracked to her home but never found her.

After the kidnapping of the Lewis children, sentiment against the Indians grew more hostile. Finally, the natives were rounded up and marched to the Round Valley Reservation, on the coast near Mendocino. Many men, including Bidwell, argued with a mob of citizens who wanted to kill the Indians. This group, of course, gathered at Pence's ranch. They didn't want to let the Indians go to Round Valley. Over 400 people were removed from the area in 1863.

After the round-up and walk, many native people flocked to Bidwell's farm for jobs, food, and survival. They were a mixture of Clear Lake, Wintun, Yana, Maidu from the valley, and Maidu from the hills. Over 250 Indians took refuge on the Bidwell Ranch. Regardless of Bidwell's motives, his actions ensured the survival of the Mechoopda Indians and those who had joined the Mechoopda after other tribes had been disrupted and scattered.

Rancho Chico

The last serious outbreaks of Indian violence happened in 1865. Nine natives killed a man and two women and robbed a home in the Concow area. A posse followed them into the hills and believed that they had killed all but one of the Indians. Later in the year, Indians attacked and robbed a party of Chinese miners on Fairfield Bar. In response, a group of men, led by Hi Goode, raided the Mill Creek Camp and killed 36 Indians. It was thought that the leader, Big Foot, died of wounds after the raid, since his footprints were never seen again. It was the last sighting of the mountain Maidu bands until 1911 when the Ishi, believed to be the last of the Mill Creek Maidu, wandered out of the hills and into the city of Orville nearly 40 years later.

The following are different accounts of the same era of turmoil and upheaval in and around Chico. The Nome Lakee reservation in Tehama had closed in 1863, and all Indians were being sent over the coastal mountain range to the Round Valley Reservation in Covelo, near the coast. The group from Chico prepared to march the Mechoopda, and other local bands of Indians, to Covelo:

> . . . A meeting of evil-disposed persons was lately held near here (Pence's Ranch), at which it was resolved to exterminate all Indians found in Butte County at the expiration of thirty days. The thirty days will expire on 27th instant, and I respectfully request that I may be instructed how to proceed in the event of a collision.
>
> —Captain Alfred Morton, United States Army, August 1863

> The soldiers came on horses and set the West People's (the Maidu) roundhouses on fire. If anyone ran away, the soldiers shot him, and if they didn't run away they probably shot him anyway. . . .
>
> —Coyote Man, 1863

On June 27, 1863, a meeting was held at the Pence ranch, 2 miles from the Lewis home. The Indian hunts began. Many natives, whose leaders had signed the treaties in 1851 and who had worked with white men, were killed. Many Indians were killed who were not perpetrators of crimes. An army of ranchers and soldiers had gathered to rid Butte County of the Indians. They were angry about the capture and killing of the Hickok and Lewis children. They felt the Indians were a threat they could not live with.

In August of 1863, Camp Bidwell was established at the Bidwell Ranch. It was manned by 102 enlisted men. Captain Ambrose E. Hooker was the commanding officer. The enraged and frightened citizens rounded up 435 Indians, with the help of federal soldiers, and brought them to Camp Bidwell. Ever enterprising, John Bidwell allowed most of the natives to camp on his land, and he also made use of their stay, hiring them as farm laborers to pick fruit, among other things.

An escort to the Round Valley Reservation near Covelo on the coastal side of the mountains was arranged, with Captain Starr as the leader. Before the group left, Bidwell appointed a special group, mostly Mechoopda, to run and hide in the river and in the caves by it. He was able to keep some of these Indians on his ranch, first by making an agreement with the superintendent of Indian Affairs, Hanson, and later by entering into contracts for labor with the natives, as advised by Hanson. Raphael, an employee of Bidwell's, was a liaison. He told the natives in hiding when it was safe to come out and threw food to them from a boat. Angry ranchers and settlers in the area threatened John Bidwell's life and property many times during this period.

On September 4, 1863, Captain Augustus Starr, with 23 soldiers under his command, left Chico with 461 Indians and 14 citizen wagons in tow. They began a 100-mile journey, known as the Nome Cult Trail, over rough terrain to the western side of the coastal mountains. Nearly half of the 461 Indians perished from hardships on the trail. On the route, 32 died of harsh conditions, and 150 were left behind, too weak or sick to make it. Two Indians escaped. On September 18, the group arrived at the Nome Cult, Round Valley Reservation with only 277 natives. Here, soldiers left the Indians for the winter with insufficient supplies.

This scenario of the march of the native people, escorted by soldiers, to a reservation in which a large percentage of the natives perished en route, due to conditions of poor water and food supply, extreme weather, and other adverse conditions, was repeated throughout the nation with many other tribes. The Mechoopda suffered the fate of their brethren with the influx of American settlers. Those left behind on the Bidwell Ranch fared better.

Mrs. Bidwell told of the cruel treatment the Indians received on this walk. She learned of their stories from natives in their employ. Santa Wilson and Mary Azbill were Indians who were both born on this trail and later came to live on the Bidwell Rancheria.

The Round Valley Reservation still exists today, and some Native Americans have made it their home. However, after the Civil War ended in 1865, escaping natives were rarely returned to the reservation. Most of the Chico natives who survived eventually made it back home. By 1864, the Bidwell Indians had extended to include some members of nearby tribes, although the Mechoopda were always the largest portion of the Indians living on the ranch. Many Mechoopda preferred to live on the Bidwell Ranch, rather than the reservation, although they missed their own way of life, their customs, and the freedom they had enjoyed previous to the arrival of the white settlers.

Like the events so rapidly unfolding in California, John Bidwell's life was also to take a new, important turn. He was, by his own account, a farmer. He believed agriculture was the cornerstone of the good life. He was drawn to public and community affairs, but his deepest interest was farming. Bidwell says of his first farming ventures, "Farming necessarily followed mining, because the mining created a demand for farm products. We immediately began raising more and more wheat, more cattle and horses. I furnished flour to the mines, and the Valley generally."

Diversity was the hallmark of Bidwell's ranch, which became a model of modern farming with its produce winning top honors at competitions. He pioneered changes in methods of agriculture within the state and pondered the thought of transportation creating a broader market:

> I believe the floods can be prevented by building reservoirs to retain the waters in the mountains, and by raising levees along the rivers. Channels must be cut to conduct the waters to dryer lands. Streams can be made available for irrigation. I look upon the future of agriculture in California to depend largely on irrigation. You can substitute irrigation for showers, and literally purple the landscape with ripening fruits. . . . It is essential for us to improve all possible ways of transportation. This once out-of-the-way land of ours is soon to become one network of rails, wires, and locomotives. And as these checker the

continent, so are steam and sail to streak the ocean. Multitudes have come and are coming to swell our population. Progress seems stamped upon the very face of things; it is the life and spirit of the age.

Bidwell raised wheat and built a flour gristmill. He also grew fruit, hay, barley, and oats. The fruit included fig, peach, apple, quince, pear, and grape.

In 1861 the Civil War began, and with it came an increased demand for western wheat. In 1860, Bidwell exported half a million barrels of wheat flour from his mill. He purchased a steamboat and transported goods and passengers from Chico to Red Bluff, along the Sacramento River, as an aide to commerce. Chico was the site of the first agricultural fair in the county. Credit was given to John Bidwell for promotion of the production of agriculture in the area. In the 1860s, Bidwell subdivided some of his land and sold parcels, large and small, to families who wanted to farm.

The rise of agriculture was also the rise of Chico. J.J. Morehead, a banker and rancher with an estate in Chico, shipped five railroad cars of wheat per day from his property during harvest season in 1873, then retired to his elaborate estate off River Road. Daniel Bidwell, John's half brother, and many other farmers, were cashing in on the fabulous wheat crops of the 1860s and 1870s in the Chico area. Fence laws were passed, and ranchers had to barricade their cattle.

Wheat continued to be the big crop in Chico until the bottom fell out of the market in 1877. A harvest in excess of three million bushels had been produced. The failure of wheat sales in bad weather eventually resulted in the division of farmland into smaller parcels, diversifying crops, planning of drainage and irrigation, along with more citrus growing, irrigation, and orchards. In 1877, land was selling for $25 to $50 per acre.

On April 28, 1888, figures in the *Chico Weekly Chronicle* indicated that there had been over 50,000 citrus plantings, mainly in Palermo and Thermalito. A fruit cannery was built in Chico in the 1880s. In 1850, there were approximately 250 peach trees in all of Butte County. By 1863, there were 150,000. The miners liked peaches, ate them, and planted the pits. Farmers were hiring Japanese and Chinese labor to pick fruit. This was one of the causes, mentioned earlier, for poor racial relations in Chico.

Judge Pratt at the Aguas Frias Rancho, south of Chico, owned the first almond ranch in 1875. Mr. Epperson and Mr. Durham did the first commercial planting in 1895. They didn't have enough suitable land until more of Aguas Frias Rancho was available by the sale of land in 1906. Durham and other almond growers formed an Almond Growers Association in 1909, and in 1918 they became affiliated with the California Almond Growers Association.

The Department of Agriculture located the Plant Introduction Gardens in Chico, in 1904, four years after John Bidwell's death. There, plants from foreign lands were introduced to Chico to observe how well they could be grown locally. Chico was chosen for its seasonal rainfall and temperate climate, and also its deep soil, well drained and fertile. The composition and texture of the Chico soil supported a wide variety of crops. Starting with 70 acres, the Plant Introduction Gardens eventually grew to over 210. Between 1898 and 1940, 140,000 varieties of plants were introduced across the nation. Out of these, 25,000 varieties were introduced in Chico.

At the Chico station, after the plants were introduced, two were planted and observed for four years while careful records were kept. If the results were favorable, they were sent to farmers to try. Fruit, nut trees, shrubs, pistachios, tung oil, jujubes, persimmons (mainly Japanese), olives, Chinese chestnuts, walnuts, almonds, apricots, plums, cherries, nectarines, and peaches were tried. Some popular varieties tested in the Chico area included: Meyer lemon, Barouni olive, Methly plum, Quetta nectarine, Lippiatt's late orange nectarine, Li and Lang jujube, and Fuyu non-astringent persimmon. The ornamentals introduced included: Chinese Holly, Carob tree, many varieties of bamboo, Nanking cherry, Dwarf peach, and 203 varieties of juniper.

During his lifetime, John Bidwell was more than a farmer; he was a statesman, a scholar, and a pioneer. Bidwell served in the U.S. House of Representatives, as a congressman from California. While he was living in Washington, D.C., the director of the Census Bureau, Joseph Kennedy, invited John Bidwell to join his family at church. He was not an active churchgoer, but he accepted the invitation. There he met Annie, Kennedy's daughter, and was smitten with her. She was beautiful. She stood a mere 4 feet, 8 inches tall, was intense, deeply religious, serene, and quiet.

John Bidwell was 46 and unmarried. He had, of course, been the target of matchmakers for years. He had succeeded in escaping all the plans made for him by friends and relatives. A decisive man and leader, Bidwell launched a campaign to win Annie's hand. She was considered a spinster at the age of 27, but she gently refused his offers. Annie was a staunch prohibitionist, and John drank alcohol and had a winery on his ranch. Neither was he devoted enough in his worship or beliefs for her liking.

In what seemed to be an earnest conversion of faith, John became a "Methodist on probation." He and Annie kept up a steady stream of letters, even while they both lived in Washington. This correspondence was to last a lifetime, as he continued to write to her during their marriage. He told her of the beautiful home he hoped to build on Rancho Chico, and his hopes that she would preside there as "queen" and make a society there, which he felt they could preside over together.

John Bidwell went home to Chico after his term without her, completely despondent. He wrote that he regretted his involvement in politics and was sincerely tired of backslapping, drinking, cigar smoking, and shady deals that went with it all. He continued to write and implore her to join him in marriage. He pulled out his wine grapes and replaced them with raisin grape varieties.

The construction of the Bidwell Mansion began in 1865, the same year Lee surrendered to the North, ending the Civil War. It was completed in 1868, and cost $60,000. The mansion was built in anticipation of Bidwell's bride, Annie Ellicott Kennedy, who had not yet consented to the marriage. However, she was destined to arrive in Chico in 1868, at the completion of her mansion home. The Bidwell Mansion was the premiere West Coast example of the Italian Villa style of architecture.

On October 7, 1867, Annie finally wrote John a letter agreeing to marriage. The wedding took place the following year. They were married in Washington, D.C. President Johnson, General Sherman, and General Grant were among the guests who attended their wedding.

Bidwell had a two-year courtship with Ms. Kennedy before their marriage, which began at a time when Bidwell was running for office again. He had served in the army and reached the rank of major. In 1849, he was named as a delegate to California's Constitutional Convention in Monterey, and in November of that year he was elected to California's first legislature as one of 16 senators. He ran unsuccessfully for reelection in 1855, but in 1865, after serving as brigadier general in the California militia during the Civil War, he was elected as a U.S. congressman to Washington, D.C., representing California. He was expected to become governor on his return to California in 1867, but this was the campaign in which his letters to Annie reflected his disillusionment with the political process. Special interests feared his unswerving idealism and his support of reforms in the public interest, such as the secret ballot, women's suffrage, public regulation of public utilities, and his anti-monopoly stance. John Bidwell's political career had already been hurt by his principles in supporting the natives and other causes. His idealism and compassion did not serve him in the political arena, and when he refrained from drinking alcohol to begin favoring Prohibitionist views, his success was further hampered.

Annie Bidwell was 29 years old when she arrived with her 48-year-old husband to the Rancho Chico and the Chico Indian Rancheria. Dorothy Hill describes Annie Bidwell at that time as well-educated, well-traveled, very religious, and from a distinguished family in Washington, D.C. She converted John Bidwell to her beliefs, for which he appeared to be grateful. She was a member of the Presbyterian Church, active in the Prohibition Party, and active in the campaign for women's rights as a member of the National Women's Suffrage Association.

Mrs. Bidwell met Nopanny, and several other Mechoopda who were employed as domestic help in John's home, at the mansion when she arrived at Rancho Chico. Soon after, she met the rest of the Mechoopda tribe who settled on their property. Her description of the village on first sight was that the homes looked like "old fashioned, dome-shaped, straw beehives."

Life was different for both the Mechoopda and for Annie after her arrival in Chico. When Mrs. Bidwell first saw the natives, they were seated on top of their dome roofs, but they quickly disappeared inside, as they vanished whenever they saw someone they didn't know. If it weren't possible to disappear, they would turn their back if they didn't know the approaching person. They did this often with Mrs. Bidwell during her first years on the ranch.

A survey dated June 27, 1860, reveals that there were 49 Indians counted in the census living on the Bidwell Rancheria. This number grew to approximately 250 Indians shortly afterward because of the persecution of the Indians at large in the Chico area. The Indians surveyed were living in three dwellings, one being the Adobe House. All of the natives living in the house were females, 11 of them, with the exception of one male, who was the chief, and the father of Nopanny. The chief, Yumarrine, was the oldest male in the tribe. The youngest person counted in this census was 16 years of age, so it is likely that children of younger ages were not accounted for in the census. The oldest Mechoopda was a female, 69 years of age.

John Bidwell had good relations with the Mechoopda and there were, no doubt, compromises made on both sides with living and working arrangements, but he did not try to change the way they worshipped or any of their traditional practices that we know of. This was not the case, however, with his new wife Annie.

Shortly after Annie's arrival, there were several funerals, and the wailing accompanying each one was disturbing to her. She suggested to her husband that it might be disturbing to others on the Rancho. Therefore, a third location of the village was devised, both to give the Indians more land, and to remove the village proceedings from under the master bedroom of the mansion. In March of 1869, the village was moved to 1 mile from the Bidwell Mansion, still further west, and about a five-minute walk from the creek. The Mechoopda village on the ranch was called the "Bidwell Rancheria," although on maps the name appears as the "Mechoopda Subdivision of the Bidwell Rancho."

Mrs. Bidwell noted that she never saw native parents strike their children or scold them, and that native children were well mannered in her home. She often took some of the children to eat lunch with her in the mansion after church services.

CHICO

Annie attended dances on the Rancheria and recorded her own description of what she saw. She relates that she was given the "place of honor" near the door. The surroundings were simple, with a dirt floor and columns supporting the domed roof. In the center a fire was kept burning. According to Annie's description, the person tending the fire was a wild-eyed fellow, who continually threw little twigs and such on the flames to keep them burning brightly. He moved his head around and chanted as he tended the fire. He wore trousers and no shirt. A piece of hair was drawn between his eyes and he often looked at it cross-eyed. Annie adds that the fire tender was sometimes portrayed as a clown.

A group of men in the secret society of Kuksu sat with their backs to the fire. They wore red, woodpecker feather helmets, with a mass of hawk feathers at the very back. The women wore white clothing, which was trimmed around the bottom with red calico. Annie left the premises at 11:30 p.m. while the dance continued.

There are many accounts and stories indicating the relationship that slowly grew between Annie and the Mechoopda Indians. That she attended the dances, observed the customs, and asked questions to find out the meanings of the Mechoopda customs indicated her great interest to understand. According to the account in the newly released book, *The Indians of the Chico Rancheria*, by Dorothy Hill, Annie Bidwell discussed the invitation to the dances with her husband, who indicated it might not be a good idea for her to go. She went though, and she protested that by better understanding the natives she could help them more. Perhaps John had not attended dances. We don't know whether his warning to Annie was a protective gesture or a stance of distance from the natives, but Annie's motives were clear. She wanted to help, even at risk to herself, so she did attend.

Mrs. Bidwell began to address the needs of the native people. She spent seven unsuccessful years trying to teach them new skills and helpful things. Finally, she started a sewing class that was a big hit. She taught them to make clothing, demonstrating how to keep clothes clean and how to do fancy stitching. She enlisted the help of the Ladies Missionary Society of the Chico Presbyterian Church in this instruction, but was soon left alone by all of the women in the group and had to tackle the task on her own. She did not give up. Annie Kennedy Bidwell taught Christianity, temperance, and formal education to the natives in their own village.

She taught the Mechoopda children to read using charts and pictures. She became a Presbyterian pastor in 1879 to perform Christian rights and ceremonies for the natives in a little church on their property, built by her husband and the native employees. After eight years she had her first convert, a male cousin of Nopanny named Tokeeno. He recovered from an illness, having been treated by Mrs. Bidwell, and said he had "died" and was sent back to earth to help finish the church and send his people to it.

In 1881, John Bidwell published a set of "rules" to be followed by the natives who wished to live on his property, which included no alcohol or drinking. At the time, Bidwell did something unprecedented. He chose Holi Lafonso as chief. Never before had this choice been made by someone from outside the native culture. John Bidwell also appointed Billy Preacher as chief teacher.

Around this time Mrs. Bidwell was of the opinion that little prejudice was felt against the Indians in public school. The Mechoopda brass band was popular in town. They played for a dozen or more years, mostly in the late 1880s. Mrs. Bidwell bought all the instruments and paid for the first lessons for the Mechoopda musicians. Later, the Indians paid $12 per week for their own lessons. On July 4, 1895, there was a Mechoopda band in a parade, an oration by Dick Phillips, an Indian from Petaluma, a display of Mechoopda articles in the Church house, and a grand reception of the Indians in town. Mrs. Bidwell felt well repaid for her hard work by the town's reaction to these festivities.

It was also noted that the Mechoopda had a great affection for each other and that their willingness to care for one another kept them from becoming rich. The natives had a great devotion to Mrs. Bidwell and would not leave the reservation without taking leave of her. When they felt an injustice was occurring, they came to her and tried to help her understand. Then she would advocate for them or try to help them understand the happenings of the white society, depending on what was more appropriate. When John Bidwell died at age 81 of a heart attack, four Indian men on the Rancheria were his pallbearers.

Billy Preacher and Amanda Wilson recorded some of the practices of the Mechoopda. The details of the first, and second, men's initiation rites, the dances, and songs were recorded. They relayed some details to Kroeber, an anthropologist from Berkley, in the early 1900s. Ethnographers Dixon, in 1899–1903, Kroeber, in 1909–1910, and Curtis in 1924, gathered a body of knowledge relevant to the Mechoopda, interviewing them on the Bidwell Rancheria. There were not many artifacts left in the culture, since all the belongings of the people who died were burned at his or her death.

Annie Bidwell performed 50 years of missionary work with the Mechoopda. They were the largest nucleus of the northwest Maidu culture in the 1900s and remain a strong group today. They called themselves the "Hulhuli'm Bahpki," which meant unsifted or mixed village, since members of their group were also from other bands of natives with basically the same or similar dialects. Their most common link, however, was their refuge on the Bidwell Rancheria. A large percentage of the group was Mechoopda. It was the largest non-reservation Indian community in the nation at the time, but was not listed in scholarly works because it was not an original land site.

Very few Mechoopda completely assimilated to the white man's way of life. They were somewhat fortunate to be able to live in a world between their own traditions and the white men's traditions during the lifetime of the Bidwells. There were some exceptions, like Bud Bain, who took up commercial fishing in the Sacramento River and raised hops for sale, and Billy Preacher, who tried to show the others an acceptance of Christianity and a new path for a modern Mechoopda existence in a new society. Not many Mechoopda left the old traditions to take up Christian beliefs, although a strong anti-alcohol group in favor of temperance formed.

Annie was vice president of the National Indian Association after the turn of the century and wrote to Senator Perkins in support of a bill before Congress, which would allow land to be granted to Indians. She expressed an opinion that they could be considered "among our best citizens, if they had land of their own for their homes, and had other political, educational, and social restrictions withdrawn." She carried out her husband's plan to distribute land to the natives. On June 4, 1909, she issued certificates of title for lots on the rancheria to individual Indians. None were recorded with the county clerk. One has been saved, the title given to Mr. and Mrs. Santa Wilson, which states:

> In consideration of $1.00, I hereby grant and convey to Mr. and Mrs. Santa Wilson, of Me-choop-da Village, and to their descendants and heirs during their natural lives, a tract of

land described as Lot 25 of Me-choop-da Subdivision of the John Bidwell Ranch on a map of April 30, 1900.

This subdivision was located off West Sacramento Avenue in Chico today. The rancheria land was deeded to the Board of Missions of the Presbyterian Church in trust for the Indians. This was kept in escrow during Annie's lifetime. It was on a plot plan showing 28 lots with 20 surnames. The roundhouse, or dance house, is ignored in this plot plan. Annie did not like the traditional worship and ceremonies the Indians conducted there.

A census was taken around 1909 or 1910, containing the names of the Indians on the ranch and their ages. Henry Azbill added the information of their tribal affiliations later, in 1970. There were 19 Mechoopda, 8 Konkau Indians, 6 Wintun, 3 Yana, and 1 Oroville Maidu, for total of 37 families.

At the time of the tribe's termination in 1958, the Mechoopda were all given allotments—the same as the other tribes—that were deeded over to a family member. The land allotted to tribal members over the years had become an island of poverty. Infrastructure and developments, common to the city of Chico, did not occur on the Bidwell Rancheria. The Mechoopda were suddenly forced to pay taxes and bring housing up to city code. This was more expensive than tribal members could afford. Immediately half of the lots were sold to the California State University at Chico for the development of affordable student housing, and eventually the rest were also sold. Apartments sprung up on what is now Mechoopda Avenue. There is still one piece of land there that is owned by a tribal member. When Mrs. Bidwell passed away on March 9, 1918, her will contained an additional 14 acres to be granted to the Mechoopda Indians for community use. This land is not in their possession at this time.

The cemetery remains, marking the site of the village. It was established around 1869, after the final move of the village. The graveyard is included in the Chico Heritage Association survey of historic sites, done in the early 1980s. It is still in its original condition, with the addition of some wood and wire fencing. There are ten upright markers, some of which are barely legible. Annie was not as tolerant of the Mechoopda culture and practices as John Bidwell was. Despite their differences, Annie developed a sincere affection for the Mechoopda Indians at the Rancho, which appeared to be mutual.

Chapter Five

ROADS, RAILWAYS, AND LUMBER

People tend to take roads for granted now, but in 1844 the only roads in the Chico area were along the Indian trails. There was the old Sacramento River Road, which followed the west bank of the Sacramento River for as long as anyone could remember. There was the California-Oregon road, and the Shasta-Tehama road, which came into Chico on what is today the Esplanade, a main thoroughfare of north-south traffic through north Chico to downtown. Trappers, explorers, settlers, and natives used this road frequently.

People in the north valley also depended on river travel and transport. The Sacramento was known as the western Mississippi, although there were difficulties in navigation. These problems worsened after the advent of hydraulic mining, although a lot of flooding was due to winter and spring rains and snow melt. Riverboats and barges transported supplies and items for trade as long as they could navigate. Near Chico, there was at least one landing. There could possibly have been two. The Chico Landing is mentioned in various diaries and publications. Bidwell's Landing is mentioned less frequently. They could have been the same landing, since Bidwell and Chico were somewhat interchangeable terms in those days.

In the 1860s, the state of California wanted to help develop roads for commerce and assist in the development of industry and industrial supplies. The state had limited funds for this development, and although many roads were needed, only one could be funded in Butte County. There were two possible routes for the state road at the time. One was between Marysville and Oroville, and the other was between Chico and Oroville. The road issue revived the long-standing competition between Oroville and Chico, vying to be chosen for roads and developments, funded by the state, which would enhance commerce and wealth for each of their respective communities.

In this case, the state granted a road building franchise to John Bidwell and associates in 1862. They were swayed by Bidwell's argument that there was still rich mining in Idaho. This meant many travelers back and forth between Idaho and California. With John Bidwell in the lead, a company formed in Chico called the Humboldt Wagon Road Company, which built a toll road through the mountains east of Chico. A traveler could take this road to Susanville. The route started in 1864 and it cost $65 to ride to Susanville on the "Hurricane Deck," which was atop a mule. A year later a stage service was established, from Chico to Ruby City Idaho, through Susanville.

This road was used as a stage route and came into Chico along the old Humboldt road through modern-day Chapman town. There were resting stations up this road every so many miles, and it was rumored that at the 10- and 14-mile stops there were bootlegging stills nearby where moonshine was sold. This no doubt made the route more popular to some.

It was along this road, and others in Northern California, where the San Franciscan Black Bart robbed stagecoaches. Transportation was nothing like what it is today. The hazards were innumerable. The following account was written by Chico resident Ester Patch Camper, who, in her lifetime, traveled both by stagecoach and by 747. The letter was published in the *Chico Enterprise Record* on August 3, 1986:

CHICO

Transportation in Chico reflected the events of the rest of the country; industry was driving the development of faster, more efficient transportation of goods. In Butte County, the railroad developed from the lumber industry's need to transport its product. According to Kent Stephens, author of *Matches, Flumes and Rails, The Diamond Match Company in the High Sierra*, in 1852 there were 14 sawmills in Butte County.

Flumes were built to transport logs out of the mountains. Men who had jobs riding them were sometimes hurt or killed. Dr. Newton Thomas Enloe, a daring young man in Chico, used the flumes in emergencies to get from one patient to another in the early days before railroad. A gentleman by the name of C.F. Ellsworth pioneered the flume in Northern California. It was known as "Ellsworth's Folly" until it was running and saving the lumber companies time and money. Chico eventually became the end point of three of the eleven flumes to be built in northern California.

Bidwell constructed a flume for the operation of his flourmill at the south edge of his property, yet the Chico Flume and Lumber Company was the pioneer in town in creating a flume that would transport logs. The company set up two sawmills at the headwaters of the Big Chico Creek in 1871. A flume was built along the creek to the mill, at the south end of Chico. It rose to 100 feet in some areas, had a depth of 30 inches, and a width at the top of 40 inches. An abundance of logs were accessible for milling due to its creation, and it caused a glut on the market in 1878.

The original company sold out to Sierra Flume and Lumber Company in 1875, which had become the largest single lumber enterprise in the world by 1877. Sierra Flume and Lumber expanded too fast, and in 1878, the company went bankrupt. The Coleman brothers bought the company and started a new venture, the Nevada County Narrow Gauge Railroad.

Although logging companies were buying up an enormous acreage of timberland, the industry could not log much of it without a better method to transport the logs down the mountain to the mills. C.F. Ellsworth emerged again to invent the logging tramway, or the first narrow gauge lumber railroad. The gauge was 39.35 inches, or a European meter. There were advantages to using the small gauge: it used less raw material to manufacture, it could turn on a much smaller radius, making curves and turns in the mountains much easier and less expensive, and the government taxed only the standard gauge railroads. It was more economical in every way.

Roads, Railways, and Lumber

Nonetheless, some lumber companies did use standard gauge railroads to transport their timber. Sierra operated two standard gauge railroads in the 1870s. Another one was attempted in Red Bluff, with difficulties at first, but by 1880 this plant was the largest pine manufacturing facility in the world, bringing Sierra back "on track." However, by the turn of the century, the Sierra Lumber Company, now run by the Coleman brothers, was in trouble again. The brothers determined to sell the company should an opportunity arise.

Around this time, the Barber Match Company of Ohio had joined with 11 other match companies to form a conglomerate called the Diamond Match Company. John Heard Comstock, a representative for Barber, arrived in Chico in June of 1901 to purchase timberland for the company.

The Diamond Match Company began their research and acquisition of timberland and a base for operations. Comstock sought to buy land for Diamond Match in a popular "checkerboard" strategy used by lumber companies, acquiring alternating plots of land. This would reduce their overall price but reserve many more acres, almost double that of the purchase, for their use. Since no one else could gain access, or would want to use the land while they were logging on the adjacent lots, it was a wise strategy.

On September 28, 1901, Frederick Deakin, Fred M. Clough, John K. Robinson, and Edward T. Hall came to stay at the Park Hotel in Chico. These gentlemen, with the exception of Hall, worked for Diamond Match. Deakin had an option on the Sierra Lumber Company land from the Colemans. He offered it to Diamond Match, who agreed to buy it but was not interested in buying any excess land. The group sold the Stirling City property and all the timberland to Diamond Match and formed the Chico Investment Company to divest the group of the excess property. The Chico Investment Company later became involved in the development of several tracts of land south of Chico, near the Diamond Match plant. The Davis Addition, the first and second Barber Addition, the Clough Addition, and others were annexed to the city in rapid succession, increasing the city size and population.

Fred M. Clough, also a member of the Chico Investment Company, became the first Pacific Coast manager for Diamond Match. The plant site was located at the end of what is now West 16th Street in Chico and was named Barber, after Ohio Columbus Barber, who was the company president when it began operations in Chico.

When Diamond Match determined to come to Chico, but before they opened their plant there, the other two lumber companies in town caught fire in the same year, 1903. The Sierra Lumber Company and the Griswold Lumber Company burned down within months of each other.

The Diamond Match Company bought land in what is now Stirling City and began construction for a logging camp/company town. Comstock's daughter, Nellie, and her husband, Charles Augusta Dreiss, came west in 1905. They lived in the mercantile building in Stirling City for two years and ran the business for Diamond Match. They later moved to Chico, where they owned several stores, including the Dreiss Jewelry store on the west side of Broadway, between Fourth and Fifth Streets in downtown Chico. After its opening, Nellie and Charles unfortunately converted their land holdings to stock, just before the stock market crashed, and they lost everything.

The Diamond Match Company, however, continued to thrive. It forced a British match company to sell by entering the English market and forcing prices so low that the London company could not compete. Diamond Match then made an offer to buy the Bryant and May Limited of London, enlarging their conglomerate.

The plant at Chico manufactured doors and matching doorjambs or doorframes known as sashes. The site had an engineering building, a powerhouse, a planing mill, warehouses, an office, and lumberyards.

CHICO

The Chico plant engineering department became a machine shop and foundry. A box factory was added to the enterprises and it produced wooden boxes for shipping produce. This led to the development and production of a special saw: the "California cut-off" saw, which was engineered for the box factory and for commercial sale as well. The match factory was actually the last facility to be built at the Chico plant and become operational. This was due to the fact that it was dangerous to produce matches in Chico's extreme summer weather without proper air conditioning, and also because the volume of match sales on the West Coast was lower than other areas where the company did business.

The Stirling City sawmill was built in 1904. It produced 250,000 feet of lumber a day. Expansion in Stirling City brought a veneer plant to the sawmill site. Soon, the location's lumber supply ran low. In order to avoid clear-cutting accessible property, Diamond Match purchased holdings of the Sierra Lumber Company in Butte, Tehama, and Shasta Counties. The acquisition was made in 1907 and totaled 90,000 acres of timber. The veneer plant was moved to Chico to accommodate the lumber supply arriving from the new purchases.

More home sites became necessary in Chico to house employees. Subdivisions were developed by the Chico Investment Company. Rosedale and Chapman town parcels, not owned by the Chico Investment Company, were annexed, subdivided, and sold for home sites. The Bidwell estate was convinced to sell more of his land for this development. Two-and-a-half miles north of Chico, the Esmerelda subdivision near Sacramento and Nord Avenues, which were larger and more attractive home sites, was formed from his property.

Diamond Match made a difference for Chico. It provided employment: nearly 2,000 employees at the company's peak. Diamond Match developed neighborhoods in the south part of town that were well built and well planned. The company backed the construction of the railroad from Chico to Stirling City.

The English partners of Diamond Match, Bryant and May, insisted on becoming involved with the Barber California branch of the business. This caused contention within the company. Finally, in an about face, Diamond Match purchased Bryant and May's stock to rid themselves of contending votes on the California enterprise development.

Pacific Coast Manager Clough allowed his son, Fred M. Clough Jr., to organize a railroad for transportation of logs from Magalia–Stirling City to the Chico plant. Fred Clough Jr. married Dr. Oscar Stansbury's daughter, Ellen Stansbury. He began construction of the Butte County Railroad, as it was named, but it was slow going. Although the franchise and the contracts were approved in September of 1902, the laying of track did not begin until June of 1903, yet they had only enough materials to put down 3 miles of track. It was November 2 before the track was completed and the first journey from Chico to Magalia was possible. The first California crew for Diamond Match arrived close to the completion of the railroad. Once the Butte County Railroad was completed, Diamond Match purchased the company from Fred Clough Jr.

The formation of a railroad company called the Chico & Northern Railroad Company was publicized in San Francisco newspapers. This caused excitement because people disliked the politics of the Southern Pacific Railroad and the Central Pacific Railroad, which seemed to have a strangle hold on transport in California, among other places. Butte County Railroad, and more specifically, the expanded Chico & Northern Railroad, was seen as the common man's comeback to the larger conglomerate railroads. What the public didn't know was that Butte County Railroad had agreed to sell to Central Pacific and lease the lines back even before the Chico & Northern Railroad Company was initiated.

Roads, Railways, and Lumber

Although Fred Clough Sr. often denied that Stirling City was a company town, the stockholders of the mercantile were, without exception, executives for Diamond Match. There were legal struggles over a monopoly on the sale of liquor in town. The company bar, the Red Devil, was the only establishment able to get a liquor license. In 1906 when Jack West, a grocery store owner, tried to obtain a liquor license, he was defeated by Major A.F. Jones, Diamond's attorney. In this and many other instances, it appeared Diamond Match was a law unto itself, especially in Stirling City. Less than a year after Jack West's defeat, a Supreme Court ruling tried to put the brakes on this type of business monopoly.

Diamond Match hoped to make a resort out of Stirling City. When the Butte County Railroad first went into operation, the company executives planned and carried out "excursions" designed to entice people to buy cabin sites or home sites and use the railway to commute to the valley. The first excursion was called "Back to the Woods," where the railroad carried 150 people to Stirling City for picnicking and sightseeing. These excursions became more popular, but few people bought home or cabin sites. The largest excursion ever was on July 4, 1910, when the railroad brought 3,000 people to Stirling City for an Independence Day celebration. A publication called *Pine Chips* promoted properties in Stirling City. However, the overall plan did not work, people continued to settle lower in the valley, and the railroad continued to operate at a loss.

Originally backed by Diamond Match Company, the Chico Electric Railroad was organized to provide streetcar transportation in the growing town of Chico and the surrounding area. The township had a population of 4,739 in 1900 and was well on its way to the 11,775 determined in the 1910 census. Petitions for a franchise were submitted both to the city and the county in December of 1903. Diamond Match executives were behind this venture but sold their shares even before the franchise was obtained. However, Fred Clough Jr. built, and even managed, the streetcar system for a short time, and the Diamond Match Company lent labor, executive power, and other resources to the venture.

Laying of track started November 2, 1904. In 1906, the company was sold to the Northern Electric Company, which was built by tycoon Henry Butters. Butters' home, south of Chico, is now a bed and breakfast called 'The Palms." Henry Butters was building track south to connect Chico with Sacramento and eventually the Bay area. Chico Electric was bought to become part of this system. The Northern Electric Company built its depot at First and Main. It also established a line up to Oroville and back from Chico, which was popular. Its tracks crossed the Southern Pacific Railroad tracks at the Southern Pacific Depot on Fifth Street and Orange. The streetcar company continued service in Chico until World War II.

The formation of railway companies happened in a flurry in Butte County and surrounding areas. Some were only paper railroads, but all companies served to hasten the establishment of rails, as well as make money for the men who established them. These railways were:

The California and Oregon Railroad was completed as far as Chico in 1870. A huge celebration was held on July 4 when the tracks reached Chico. Gridley, Biggs, and Durham were towns that resulted from railroad passage through these areas. This is the line that goes through Chico today, but Central Pacific controlled it by the time it reached Chico in August of 1870. It was actually controlled by the owners of Central Pacific since at least 1868, or earlier. The Marysville Railroad was proposed to build from Roseville to Oregon, and they incorporated in 1867. Then the California-Oregon Company of 1865 proposed to construct from Marysville to Roseville in 1867, but they did not do either. Finally, the California Central of 1857 did in fact build a line from Folsom, north through what is now Roseville to Lincoln; the company was consolidated into the California-Oregon Railroad of 1868, which was then controlled by the Central Pacific Railroad. The rails between Folsom and Roseville were removed, but the rails through Chico still remain. Prior to 1870, Chico's outlets to the north consisted mainly of the Shasta road and an outlet to the Sacramento River, 6 miles west of town. This railroad eventually became the Southern Pacific north/south mainline from Roseville into southern Oregon.

The Yuba Railroad was constructed between 1862 and 1868. It was controlled by Central Pacific Railroad from 1867 to 1868, which consolidated in 1869 into the California-Oregon Railroad of 1868. It didn't go all the way to Marysville, but the line was completed through Chico between May and July of 1870, as the California-Oregon Railroad.

The Diamond Match Company Railroad was organized on August 8, 1902. It was steam operated on standard gauge and 39.35 gauge. It was located in Stirling City. The railroad was built to Butte Falls, a distance of 45 miles. Most of this trackage was 39.35-inch narrow gauge. Two other lines were planned but not built from Nelson, on the Southern Pacific, to the timber (a distance of 31 miles) and from Durham, on the Southern Pacific (30 miles north of Marysville), to Cherokee Ditch, Little Butte Creek, and on up to the timber. The standard gauge section was abandoned in 1952, and the last rail was removed in July 3, 1953.

The Butte County Railroad Company was established in 1902. The franchise was granted in November 11, 1902 and was located in Chico. The company was incorporated on February 24, 1903. Construction began in April of 1903. Regular service between Barber and Magalia began November 2, 1903. The railroad opened for traffic to Stirling City April 15, 1904. It was sold to the Central Pacific Company, who then transferred to the Southern Pacific Company in November 27, 1903. Southern Pacific leased back the tracks to the Butte County Railroad Company for operation. Butte County Railroad Company dissolved January 21, 1916. Then trackage went back through the Central Pacific to the Southern Pacific again, and was then known as Southern Pacific Chico–Sterling City Branch. The Butte County Line was absorbed into Southern Pacific.

The Kimshew Railroad Company ran from 1910 to 1912. Kimshew and the Diamond Match Railroad Companies supplied logs from the woods to the mill in Stirling City. The Butte County Railroad brought cut lumber from the mill in Stirling City down to the Barber plant in Chico.

The Chico & Northern Railroad Company was incorporated on November 11, 1903. The company was said to be located in Chico; however, it had been incorporated by the Southern Pacific Company only as a holding company for the properties of the Butte County Railroad Company, a standard gauge, steam-operated railroad. The route was to be the same as Butte County Railroad—Chico to Magalia and back, a distance of 30.57 miles each way. When the Butte County Railroad Company was completed, Southern Pacific leased the property back to them. Butte County Railroad was the only asset that Chico & Northern ever held, since it had been created only to lease the Butte County Railroad line. The Chico & Northern dissolved February 29, 1912. Southern Pacific acquired the Chico & Northern, as planned, and ran until the rails were removed in the 1980s.

The Chico Electric Railway Company incorporated on August 15, 1904. It was, of course, electric and a standard gauge operation. The company built 4.5 miles of street railway in Chico. It began operations on January 1, 1905 and was sold to Northern Electric Company on August 1, 1905, when a line from Chico to Oroville, and on to Sacramento, was about to be established.

The Northern Electric Company incorporated in 1905 and later became the Northern Electric Railway Company in 1907. This was the paper part of the Northern Electric Railway Company. A route from Oroville to Chico was planned when the railway was still Chico Electric and was completed in 1906. Northern Electric acquired the Chico Electric Railway Company, adding some miles to the line and operating 5.14 miles of street railway in Chico. The company was deeded to the Northern Electric Railway Company on December 2, 1907. It was sold to the Sacramento Northern Railroad April 18, 1918.

The Northern Electric Railway Company incorporated on September 19, 1907, and the railway was electric and standard gauge. It became the Northern Electric Railway Company, located in Chico. It was organized solely to take over the properties of the Northern Electric Company on December 2, 1907. On May 15, 1909, it purchased the Shasta Southern Railway Company with a distance of 5.73 miles. The Sacramento & Woodland Railroad Company was acquired on June 13, 1912 at a distance of 17.3 miles, and the West Side Railroad was purchased in 1912, with a distance of .498 mile. The Northern Electric Railway Company created a Marysville & Colusa Branch in 1910. In December of 1912, it purchased the properties of the Vallejo & Northern Railroad Company. It was finally sold to the Sacramento Northern Railroad June 28, 1918. It eventually ran through Durham, Oroville, and Marysville to Sacramento.

The Sacramento Northern Railroad Company route was from Oakland to Chico through Marysville, after consolidation with the Oakland-Antioch & Eastern. It later operated passenger and freight trains down Chico Main Street to the depot. Passenger service was abandoned in 1939, but the tracks went down the Esplanade and Main Street in the 1970s, still carrying freight. The Oakland-Antioch & Eastern, (also known as the Oakland-Antioch or the San Francisco–Sacramento Short Line) connected with the Northern Electric (absorbed into Sacramento Northern) in Marysville. Both companies operated under Western Pacific in the late 1920s. The Oakland-Antioch and Eastern crossed the San Francisco Bay via ferryboat until the Bay Bridge was completed. The Sacramento Northern was one of three electric companies to operate trains across the bridge. Sacramento Northern stopped passenger service a few years after completion of the bridge and became strictly a freight railroad, except for local streetcar operations.

The Southern Pacific Railroad Company had its current depot building built in Chico in 1892. It was the western half of the first Transcontinental Railroad. It took over its corporate predecessor, Central Pacific. Southern Pacific went from Sacramento to Promontory Point, Utah. These railroads were built and operated by the Big Four. The corporations owned by these men were not popular with the common people, who wanted to see their local companies succeed. Big railroads ruthlessly swallowed up little railroads faster than they could go into business, if their routes were viable and business was good. Southern Pacific eventually owned every railroad worth owning in the north valley. Union Pacific bought out Southern Pacific in 1996 and is the railroad that currently runs through Chico.

The Western Pacific Railroad Company went through the Oroville and Feather River Canyon, through Beckworth Pass. In 1910, it opened passenger service to Oroville. Western Pacific selected Oroville for its Roundhouse site. The Roundhouse was built there to be used for storing, repairing, and switching locomotives for the company. It was the last transcontinental route. It was purchased by Southern Pacific, then immediately bought out by Union Pacific. Impending mergers were announced in January 1980 and, in 1982, it became the fourth operating district of Union Pacific. In 1985, it was renamed the Feather River District.

The Union Pacific Railroad Company bought the Southern Pacific in 1996. Its origin was the eastern half of the 1869 Transcontinental Railroad that drove the gold spike at Promontory Point, Utah, in 1869. Central Pacific, which became Southern Pacific, was the other half of the Transcontinental Railroad. From a functional point of view, the Central Pacific and the Southern Pacific were one management organization. They were jointly owned and operated cooperatively but forced apart by anti-trust laws in 1913. Union Pacific owned lines in the Los Angeles area in 1901 and continued to acquire lines throughout the century.

The California Northern Railroad Company, the nineteenth century company of the 1860s, was reorganized as the Northern California Railroad in March 1, 1885, controlled by Southern Pacific Railroad. The first line opened in 1864 and ran between Marysville and Oroville only. It was originally steam powered. By 1915, it would be listed as the Southern Pacific, leased to the Southern Pacific Railroad Company in June of 1889, and consolidated in 1898. Eventually, it built a line to Knight's Landing, replacing a California Pacific line that had been washed out. In 1971 it was leasing lines from Union Pacific. California Northern did green runs, which were short runs for produce and were frequent in the central valley.

Oro Dam Constructors Railroad Company was organized for building the Oroville Dam in October 1962. It was a diesel, standard gauge railroad, located in Oroville. It was built from the dam site to the quarry. The main line trackage was 11.65 miles and the total was 19.25 miles. It began operations on October 1, 1963. It made a junction with the Western Pacific Railroad at Zephyr Siding.

Other railways such as the Chico and Colusa Railroad existed, but only on paper.

The Diamond Match Company had an estimated 3.5 billion feet of standing lumber in 1908, but it was of poor quality and hard to access. A new president, Mr. Stettinus, brought in an engineer, William Armstrong Fairburn, who overhauled the company's operations. The Stirling City plant had been proposed for advanced development; however, the veneer plant was losing money, the turpentine plant and wood pulp mill had never been built, and the company could not afford to build them.

New management accelerated Clough's retirement for "a much needed rest." This was an indication that they were not on the same page. Many of the original "California Dreamers" of the company had retired or were no longer involved in the plant operations. Clough's retirement was mourned in Chico, where his high profile involvement with community development had brought him many contacts and high esteem.

The new management made a decision to cut back operations in California to help the company's financial standing. They had produced more than they could sell and their lumber was stockpiled. Even in the rising demand for lumber created by World War I, California production for Diamond Match remained low.

The Barber facilities were virtually abandoned until 1919 when the company started a millwork factory on the site. Fairburn visited the plant and made notes on the production inefficiencies. He began a corrective plan and a new office was built for the Chico plant's resumption of operation in 1920.

Safety, fire insurance, fire prevention, and planning became a bigger part of operations at Diamond Match. World War II brought higher production and increased tree replanting. It was the end of an era for the lumber industry in the Chico area. The last Stirling City Crew finished in 1959, although the Chico plant was still operating in the 1970s. Eventually, the Louisiana Pacific, which closed operations, purchased the plant and surrounding land.

It was the end of an era for the railroads also. The automobile took preference over train travel, and trucking became the preferred method of shipping freight. With these two developments, a death knell was sounded for the railroads. They lost business, became weaker and gradually dissolved, or fell into the ownership of Union Pacific.

Chapter Six

THE BUILDING ERA

The population of what is now Chico got its first big boost from the gold rush and the business that went with it. Growth did not stop with mining. Families came to California because of the dry climate. Businesses were moving west, and that meant jobs and opportunities. People also came with the railroads, or they might have bought surplus land from the railroads at a bargain price and traveled to develop it. Some came to acquire land for farming or ranching. Although gold was still big business through the 1890s, it tapered off after the 1860s, and Chico's official start in 1860 attracted people and families that were seeking other resources.

The area began construction in the early 1850s. Before the city of Chico was established, Bidwell and a few others built near the future site of the city. In 1853, Bidwell assembled the first flour gristmill in the area, and possibly the second gristmill in northern California. It was across from his home, on the north bank of Big Chico Creek. He sold flour and wheat to the mines. There were taverns, a few homes, and, of course, Bidwell's two-story adobe home, which also served as a way station for travelers.

Other farmers or ranchers built home estates similar to John Bidwell's. These were scattered throughout the north valley. Some of these estates, close to Bidwell's ranch, were the home of Squire Wright (later known as the Patrick Ranch) located on the road from Chico to Sutter's Fort, and J.J. Moorhead's estate on River Road, part of Chico today. Peter Lassen was in the present-day town of Vina, but John's half brother, Daniel Bidwell, lived closer. Daniel was up the Shasta-Tehama Road about 3 miles, in Sandy Gulch, where the Miller Mansion is now. Today, Sandy Gulch is Lindo Channel, a part of Chico. Samuel Neal had a big ranch south of town, as did Manoah Pence. There were many more settlers, some doctors, some laborers, and some looking for land to subsist on.

The 1858 Lincoln-Douglas Debates put a strain on the relations of newly-formed communities in California. Some settlers in the Chico area were southerners and sided with Douglas, but most were northerners and sided with Lincoln. The North was in favor of westward expansion, the acquisition of more states to the Union, and more land. The South, steeped in agriculture and not privy to the industrial gains of the North, balked as new "free" states came into the country. Dread built as they watched the scales of the country's economic system tip further and further to their disadvantage.

After Lincoln was elected President, the South seceded from the Union and soon a Civil War ensued. The sympathies of the majority of Butte County residents were with the Union in the Civil War. Some men enlisted in the Union Army and a military camp was set up on the Bidwell property. Men from Butte County joined with other soldiers in the Union Army to defend California if needed. They took it upon themselves to keep Southern sympathizers quiet and under control. Some of these men were sent to Humboldt County and Arizona. John Bidwell served as a general in this militia, but that did not deter him from proceeding with plans for the community.

CHICO

Chico was the scene of much celebration after the northern victory. Of course, the death of Lincoln was deeply mourned and memorial services were held. Later, when the Chico Vecino subdivision north of town was created and annexed to Chico, a street near the Bidwell residence was named Lincoln Avenue.

John Bidwell was not the first white settler in the Chico area, but he was certainly one of the earliest and the person with the greatest and longest impact on the city of Chico. He owned the land the city was built on. As soon as his land was surveyed and he received the certificate of patent for Rancho Chico, from the commissioner of the land office in San Francisco in April 1860, he commissioned County Surveyor J.S. Henning to create a plan for the Chico town site consisting of 50 blocks, laid out between Big Chico Creek and Little Chico Creeks.

The "laying out" of Chico occurred 12 years before it became incorporated, and building in the area started even before that. The newly planned town was centered on the Shasta-Tehama Road, which became Main Street in town and the Esplanade north of town. Probably because Bidwell was a Mason, the town was laid out in a diamond shape, pointing north. As a result, downtown streets do not run true north and south, nor east and west. They are all on the diagonal. The present day social and economic center of town remains the same as the one Bidwell and Henning laid out. Over the past 143 years, Chico has grown from a farm community of less than 500 to the present metropolitan community of over 100,000.

The town site lay between the two creeks. The north boundary was First Street, and on the south, Sixth Street. The east boundary was Wall Street, and the west boundary was Sycamore (now Normal Avenue). The town consisted of 50 blocks. The first few buildings went up quickly, and all claim to be first. A saloon built by Duncan Neal, an early store built of brick by E.B. Pond, and the Bidwell Building were built in 1861. Richard Breese possibly built the first "home," since he lived in his office where he ran an express delivery business for the California Steamboat Navigation Company. The boats were running daily, up the Sacramento River, from Sacramento to Red Bluff and back. Breese delivered goods brought to Chico by steamboat.

At first there were far more men than women and a lot of gambling and drinking. As women came to town and it became home to more families, Chico became more respectable. Bidwell actively recruited people of good character and influenced them to buy lots and settle in Chico, in order to build up a reputable town. The more he wanted someone to settle in the town, the cheaper the price of the lot became. Some were given to foremen on his ranch or other people he held in high regard. Bidwell's wide streets, tree-lined and spacious, gave flexibility and peacefulness to a relatively small community. His gifts to the town included land for churches, schools, a city plaza, and for the city's municipal use, among other things. He gave each denomination a city block to build a church on. In 1870, there were seven established churches.

By 1869, Chico had 2,500 people. The town had a school on land donated by John Bidwell. He sold a lot of land on block 81 for $1 to Woodman's Academy, and a school was built on the lot on Fifth Street. The Academy on Fifth Street became a private school in the late 1800s.

The Italian villa–style Bidwell Mansion was also constructed during this time. The first story was 15 feet high, the second 12 feet, and the attic 11 feet. The home had 54 rooms. There was 17,000 surface feet of flooring, and it had a basement. A cistern in the upper part of the building furnished every room with water. Bidwell's ranch was a showplace in the state. Eventually, 55 buildings were erected on the ranch, including ten barns. He built an observatory and water towers near the mansion. In 1877, a large fruit drying facility was constructed. One mile from his house was the Rancheria where at least 100 Indians lived. Bidwell provided medical care, a Presbyterian chapel, and an educational facility for them. Thirty Indian men, or more, were wage earners on Bidwell's property.

He also built a general store in town on the corner of First Street and Broadway, where the Tres Hombres restaurant is today. This was in the two-story Bidwell Building, which also served as the post office and his business office as well. The story of the Chico Post Office is a long saga.

The first post office in the area was in John Bidwell's adobe house, on the north bank of Big Chico Creek. It then moved into the Bidwell Building, which was built in 1861. Later it moved to the Masonic–Odd Fellows Lodge/Hardware Store, now Collier's Hardware, (corner of First Street and Broadway, across the street from the Bidwell Building). The hardware store was built in 1871. A new post office was being planned fronting the downtown plaza on Fifth Street, but it wasn't finished, so the Chico Post Office was moved out of the hardware store onto Second Street. When the new building was completed, they finally moved the post office to where is today, on Fifth and Broadway.

The Chico Brewery at Eighth and Broadway was advertised in the local paper. Charles Croissant Bavarian, a brew master, bought the half block the brewery stood on for $1 from John Bidwell in 1874. He tore down the existing building, constructed in 1865, and rebuilt the present structure in 1874. The brewery served ale, lager, and porter for more than 25 years. In the rear, there was a saloon and card room. The second floor was a boarding house. It contained many businesses, including Pullins Cyclery. Now it houses a restaurant and deli. Some of the side windows have been bricked in.

Oakdale School was built on the south bank of the Little Chico Creek, which was not Bidwell land. Mrs. L.L. Sproul conducted the first classroom in Chico in 1861, in a house on a farm where Oakdale School was later built. The school building was in use from 1874 to the late 1940s.

An exciting modern-day project in the Chico area is an historic home site on the Midway, the road between Durham and Chico, which is currently considered the area's oldest standing structure. The foundation dates back to 1853 or before. The ranch house is located just south of Chico, at Hegan Lane and the Midway.

Originally, the land that the ranch house was built on was part of the Agua Nieves Mexican Land grant. This claim was denied when it came time to prove claims, and the land was purchased by James Marshall. The Patrick Ranch Council research shows Thomas "Squire" Wright, justice of the peace in Chico, as buying the land for his ranch from John Bidwell. He came in 1849, over the Lassen Trail, on his way to Sutter's Fort, but he liked the Chico area and stayed. He came with three men, by oxen, and they spent the first winter on the Feather River. He tried to buy the Compton/Northgraves place, just to the south of where he built, but it was spoken for, so he bought the property to the north.

Squire first built a hotel on the Shasta-Oroville Road, on the west edge of large grove of oak trees, which was an Indian Rancheria. The building was moved to where it is now. It has also been added on to and made into a family residence. Squire Wright died and left his estate to his wife, his son, and his sister Melissa. When Melissa's husband William Garrison Patrick died six years later, as a widow she continued living and working on the ranch. Darrell Deter, the great-grandson of Melissa Wright Patrick, has retold some of this story from memory. He mentioned that his great-grandmother went back east to visit her family after her husband passed away. When she came home, she was traveling on the same boat with John and Annie Bidwell, when John was bringing his bride back to Chico. Melissa's two-year-old child sat on Annie Bidwell's lap for part of the journey. Melissa raised her six

CHICO

children, one of them William Garrison Patrick II, and took care of the ranch. She was a good businesswoman and later bought out Squire's son.

It appears the Wright-Patrick home, now called the Patrick Ranch House, had a second story added in the late 1850s when the hotel/home was moved. The home was dismantled during the process. Parts were reincorporated into the present structure; for instance, some of the windows still bear the original glass, which was shipped around the Horn. There is research in progress indicating that this first structure may have been built as early as 1849–1850. William Garrison Patrick II died at age 50, and he had three children. William Garrison Patrick III, or "Pat," was born in 1904 and at the time of his father's death was a bachelor, so he took over farming the ranch. He married Hester Grimm, at age 54.

The Patrick Ranch House was the site of the first airport in Butte County. Pat Patrick founded the airport in 1929 and was a man who was very mechanical, liked to fix everything, and loved to fly. He did his share of barnstorming and thoroughly used the airport at his ranch. The airfield was located next to the Patrick family cemetery, near the Maidu Indian Rancheria. The ranch is among the Chico area's "historical treasures, a link with the agricultural, economic, and cultural heritage, and a virtually unchanged representative of ranch life in early California."

Northgraves, another early Chico area landowner, originally made his money prospecting with Bidwell. Northgraves used the contractors that built the Bidwell Mansion for his home, just south of the Wright-Patrick Ranch. He hired a man named Bryant to run his place. The Bryants took care of Northgraves in his old age. In return, Bryant said they were to inherit the property. This claim went into litigation. The Bryants were awarded the property but lived there only a short time. Bee Patrick, the former next-door neighbor, and her husband, Adam Compton, bought the property from the Bryants. Northgraves, when he was younger, had rented a room from Squire Wright and Melissa Wright Patrick. One of Melissa's children, Bee, had watched Northgraves build his house, and had always wanted to live in it.

When Bee Patrick Compton died in 1945, she stipulated that her home (the Compton/Northgraves home) could not be inherited for 10 years. Chico State College wanted to buy the empty Compton house, but so did Pat Patrick. Warren Brusie Sr., owner of the funeral home and the Chico Cemetery and a hunting buddy of Pat's, wanted to help him. Brusie bought a huge chunk of land, which included the house and a family cemetery. The university got discouraged, and instead bought the Miller Ranch down the road for their University Farm. Pat farmed part of the land owned by Warren Brusie. Pat and Hester Patrick moved into the Compton/Northgraves home. Hester was active in the community and took interest in matters of historic preservation. She served on the committee to preserve the Honey Run Covered Bridge over Butte Creek. Upon her death, she left her home to the Chico Museum.

Another of the area's oldest buildings still standing is in downtown Chico. It was built at 824 Oroville Avenue, near Ninth Street and Park Avenue. At first it was called "Clark and Stapp's Junction," and was located at a junction where several roads reached Chico's downtown, including Humboldt Road and the Shasta-Oroville Road. Most of today's population might know the building as Cabo's or The Palms, popular bars of the recent past. It is presently a music supply store. When prohibition shut the saloon down, it became a meat market, a barbershop, a laundry, a tailor store, and then a motorcycle business. When the Congressional Act was repealed, it opened again as the T. Davis Beer Parlor.

The Building Era

The *Butte Record*, started and owned by C.W. Stiles, first published at Bidwell's Bar, was taken over by George Crosette, who was running a hotel in Oroville, and who traded his ranch and a hotel for the newspaper. When the boom ended at Bidwell's Bar, the paper moved to Oroville. In 1864, Crosette sold the paper to James Wagstaff, who ran it as the *Oroville Union Record* (no doubt because of the Civil War politics). In 1866, Crosette bought it back from Wagstaff and changed the name back to the *Butte Record*. Crosette moved to Chico in 1873 and took the *Butte Record* with him. About this time, the *Record* absorbed another newspaper publishing in town, the *Chico Chronicle*, and it became the *Chico Morning Chronicle-Record*. A gentleman by the name of C.W. Clough bought this paper in 1880 and then sold it in 1897. It changed its name again, this time to the *Chico Record*.

Several other newspapers were brewing in Chico, a town that apparently liked to read. The *Chico Index* was published in the city for a short time after it was laid out in 1860. W. Bishop published the *Chico Courant* from 1864 to 1869. The *Chico Semi Weekly Review* sprang up in 1871. The *Northern Enterprise* took over the *Chico Semi Weekly Review* in 1872, which had been published for only one year. The *Butte County Free Press* started in Chico and later became the *Chico Caucasian* because of the intense anti-Chinese feelings in town. The equipment from the *Caucasian* was sold to S.N. DeHaven, who issued the *Northern Enterprise*.

The *Northern Enterprise* changed hands, used equipment put together from different sources, and finally became the *Chico Enterprise*. Under the direction of W.C. Chalmers as editor, and Ed Hoole as proprietor, the *Chico Enterprise* became the steady competition for the *Chico Record* for over 75 years. It was the more progressive paper of the two. In 1947, Stanley and Samuel Beaubaire sold the *Chico Record* to the *Chico Enterprise*. They continued to publish as separate papers, although the same company owned them, for one year. On December 6, 1948, they became the *Chico Enterprise Record*, which is Chico's local daily newspaper today.

The town of Chico was quickly growing in the 1870s. The Chapman addition was established in 1871, and the Oakdale subdivision was added later in the 1870s. These two additional subdivisions opened settlement to the south of Chico. Another addition to the city moved the eastern boundary to Olive Street, where it remained until 1906.

On January 8, 1872, the state proposed that Chico incorporate as a city. Chico held its first municipal election on February 5, 1872, when 217 votes were cast. The first board of trustees formed in 1872, and they chose the length of their terms by lot. G.W. Dorn was elected the first president of the Board of Trustees for Chico. At that time, the contest for county seat was taken up by Chico citizens and would continue for many years. In 1872, Chico raised $25,000, of which John Bidwell supplied $10,000 for a county seat campaign. An election was held and Chico attained 1,604 votes to Oroville's 1,904, thus Chico lost the county seat race. The town would continue to lose every competition for county seat approximately once a decade thereafter. However, they did gain advantages in development by locating the northern State Normal School in Chico, and by being selected for important roadways and railways.

The first fire in Chico was at the What Cheer House in 1863. The town organized the Chico Engine Company Number 1. It was a community fire-fighting brigade with a horse-drawn fire engine. The local paper, the *Northern Enterprise*, recorded the following stories about some of the many fires in Chico:

> On December 27, 1872 a Monday, at noon, a dwelling on 2nd Street owned by C.L.
> McStilson, and occupied by E.J. Reilly, was discovered to be on fire. The cry of "Fire!"

brought out a large number of citizens eager to render all aide possible. No effort was lacking. Every fire fighter seemed to vie with the other to conquer the fire. As usual there was not a hook or ladder, not a bucket to be found, and men were compelled to standby and see the building burn to the ground. When buckets were found, it was but a few minutes until the well gave out. . . ."

An alarm was sounded east of town by the cry of "Fire! Fire!" and was located at the residence of J.H. Parr, a house painter, on Fourth Street between Flume and Orient. The bucket brigade responded and were pouring buckets of water on the blaze when J. McStilson drove up in his buckboard drawn by a pinto Indian pony, and with his Babcock fire extinguisher, put out the fire.

The city fire equipment was no match for fiery holocausts. On April 19, 1873, a serious fire in Chico began in the hayloft of the Fashion Stable at Third and Main. O.P. Weed, the proprietor, had been sleeping there. He left the building with his clothing in hand. The fire was a tragedy as 38 people died in the blaze. Citizens fought the flames all night in a line, passing buckets of water to quench the fire. It burned down everything on the entire block except one house.

Just one month before the fire of 1873, the City of Chico Board of Trustees called a meeting to organize a fire company. It was formed on April 5, but not soon enough to handle the terrible fire a few days after. On June 2, the company acquired a fire engine.

Three more major fires in the next two years did thousands of dollars of damage. In some ways, the town was like a phoenix rising from the ashes. Despair and dismay over fires and their damages were mixed with hope, tremendous growth, and hallmark events in Chico's development.

Chicoans rallied again in an attempt to secure Chico as the county seat. John Bidwell gave the first gift of land to the city for a downtown plaza park in 1874. It is still the present day City Plaza, although Oroville, not Chico, remained the county seat. On February 27, 1876, a row of frame buildings on the west side of Main between Second and Third Streets burned. Beside themselves, the citizens formed a volunteer organization to assist the city Fire Station.

The bright red shirts and black helmets of the volunteer fire department, The Deluge Hose Company, were colorful. These firemen were a hit at parades, picnics, and social activities. The wives of the firemen also put on functions for the city. On Thanksgiving of 1883, the city held the Deluge Hose Hop. A contest was held to see what company would respond quicker to a fire call, as it was held with the Red Bluff Fire Company. Chico won the contest.

In 1874, the Women's Christian Temperance Union (WCTU) organized in New York. Annie Bidwell was a supporter of women's suffrage and Prohibition and a member of the WCTU. Susan B. Anthony and Frances Willard were good friends of Annie's and visited the Bidwell Mansion from time to time. A street near Annie's mansion home was named after Frances Willard, whose political strategies in advancing the rights of women were ingenious.

While president of the Illinois Chapter of the WCTU, Frances Willard spearheaded a statewide temperance petition campaign and gained the signatures of more than 100,000 women throughout the state of Illinois. She became a model for the WCTU in the nation. In 1879, she was elected president of the national WCTU. She held this position for the rest of her life.

The Building Era

Since most women of those times were dependent on a husband's wages and were not allowed to even own property, alcoholism posed more of a threat for them at that time than it does today. Frances Willard led the largest women's organization of the nineteenth century of basically conservative, anti-political, church-going women into public action using the language of women's traditional roles to propel them forward.

Willard's "Home Protection Ballot" was a euphemistically couched platform for women's suffrage. Her "Do Everything" campaign added issues such as public kindergarten, childcare for working mothers, and facilities for dependent and neglected children to the ballot. She supported industrial job training for women, the eight-hour workday, organization of labor, and "social purity" fight against prostitution and venereal disease. She admitted that, "under the mould of conservative action, I have been most radical in thought."

Annie Bidwell contributed a reading room to the town's WCTU, which later became the city library. She supported the women's suffrage movement, education, and the political involvement of women at a time when it was crucial for the success of the West, and the nation, to incorporate the types of programs backed by so many women, including education and welfare of children.

Chico's Bidwell Mansion was a haven for lively discussions on these topics. The Bidwells often had active political and philosophical discussions in which women were allowed to take part, if they wished. The prevailing thought was that such topics would stir up women's emotions and cause physical distress. This was not the belief of the couple, and Annie participated in discussions regularly. Visitors to the mansion included relatives of the Bidwells, scientists, politicians, dignitaries, professionals, activists, anthropologists, and writers, such as John Muir.

One of the many distinguished visitors was Sir Joseph Hooker, the world's best-known botanist in those days. An enormous oak tree was growing on the Bidwell property in an area that was set aside for public use and picnicking. Sir Joseph Hooker was taken to the location of the huge oak tree. It has since been known in Chico as the "Hooker Oak." It is believed by some that the giant tree was actually two trees grown together. It had an estimated age of 1,000 years and a spread of branches 503 feet in circumference. Allowing 2 square feet per person, 8,000 people could stand under its branches. In 1921, the circumference of the Hooker Oak was 28 feet 2 inches, at 8 feet above the ground. The tree was 110 feet high, and the longest branch was 111 feet. The Hooker Oak fell in the late 1970s.

The Bidwells not only invited visitors, they also recruited people from among their relatives and acquaintances to move to town. Annie Bidwell encouraged Ella Gatchell, a cousin of John Bidwell, and her husband William to move from the East to Chico. Both of the Gatchells were physicians. Ella became Annie's personal doctor and the couple had an office in the Bidwell Building. The Gatchells then encouraged their relatives, the Cliffords, to move to Chico. The Cliffords opened a downtown jewelry store that is still doing business on Broadway today.

Late in June of 1875, Dr. Oscar Stansbury made his way to Chico from Carrollton, the county seat of Carroll County, Mississippi. His relative, Dr. George Griffiths, formerly a practicing doctor in town, was giving up his practice and retiring to the Parrot Ranch outside of town. He urged Oscar to relocate, take over his practice, become a landowner, and enjoy the West. Oscar boarded the Mississippi Central Railroad, bound for St. Louis, and from there he took the overland route to California, presumably in a wagon.

The final leg of the journey after arriving in Sacramento was by rail. He boarded the California and Oregon Railroad, heading north to Chico, 100 miles away. When he arrived he found the depot nondescript. A stage pulled up to the station with the words "Chico Hotel" on the side. He described the adventure as the stage made its way down Fifth Street, allowing us to see Chico through his eyes:

> My first impression was of a town that anticipated its own growth. We passed through a network of broad, airy streets, each block neatly laid out, as though stamped by a giant gridiron. While some blocks enclosed nothing but open fields, most were dotted with wood-framed houses, barns, and sheds, almost all painted white looking crisp and clean in the bright afternoon sun. Here and there huge sycamore offered inviting islands of shade. Around many of the blocks stood neat rows of newly planted trees. At Salem Street, the driver wheeled sharply left, and shortly came to a stop before an imposing three-story building around two-sides of which ran a rather ornate gallery, supported by slender columns resting on a wooden walkway. Inscribed on the central pointed pediment was, "Chico Hotel" and beneath it, I.A. Weatherbee.

The next morning, Stansbury went for a tour of the town, and again his impressions are fresh and revealing. He discovered the business district was confined to three blocks, running north and south, with one- and two-story offices of brick and wood. These were facing on two wide streets, Main and Broadway. It was a "quiet, rural town carved out of fields of a sea of wheat and barley. Now and then a buggy, a dray, or farm wagon passed by, moving at a leisurely pace. The occupants were relaxed and unhurried."

Doctor Stansbury started his practice at Graves Drug Store at Second and Main Streets, and worked for two years before leaving to marry his sweetheart, Libbie, and bring her to Chico to live. They arrived together in town on May 29, 1877. At first Libbie was homesick, and not very fond of this Western town. It took her quite awhile to adjust to life in her new surroundings. Dr. Stansbury wanted to move out of Chico and buy land so that he could farm a little, but Libbie did not want to do this, so they bought the lot at Fifth and Salem. In 1882, plans were drawn up for a home, for the Stansburys "that would be a credit to the community."

The Stansburys chose plans for their home drawn up by A.A. Cook of Sacramento. It was built in an Italianate style, with ornamentation, described as "a marriage of the floral and picturesque." The architect had to modify the plans to suit a doctor's needs. It had an outside entrance to a room for emergency treatment, and room for buggies and gigs parked outside. There were four bedrooms for the family, a back staircase access to the kitchen, a cool pantry for storing foodstuffs, a dumbwaiter for moving food from the cellar to the kitchen, both a parlor and sitting room, and a dining room. The contractors made pediments, cornices, entablatures, balusters, fluted columns, newels, and decorative bands. The interior had hand-carved cornice scrolls. Paperhangers from San Francisco hanged highly-patterned paper, and stenciled decoration was done on the parlor room ceiling. The house boasted gold-leaf molding, a stained glass window above the stairway, and wall-to-wall carpeting. Gas lighting fixtures, rare at the time, were installed. The house was finished in record time, by August of 1883. The gas, sewer, and water were even hooked up, and these were very modern conveniences. This is probably when Libbie stopped feeling homesick.

Oscar Stansbury seemed to be a man of integrity, with concern for good medical practice. He contributed knowledge, research, and leadership in these areas, and in other areas of civic duty, throughout his life in Chico. His comments on the status of the medical profession at the time are enlightening:

> From 1903 until 1915, I was a member of that Board [California State Board of Health]. The practice of medicine at the turn of the century was approaching a renaissance, but there still existed a frightening lack of knowledge on the part of doctors, health officers and the public as to the practice of sanitation, the causes and control of epidemics, yes, and even proper methods of preserving food. Patent medicines could be bought anywhere with no governmental control of their contents and no restrictions on sales. Physicians were prescribing opium-based drugs indiscriminately, some believing they had curative powers, but most to give relief from pain. Indeed, so little was actually known that the primary service performed by the doctor was to alleviate suffering rather than to provide a cure for illness. You may not believe it when I tell you the medical profession was so lacking in the knowledge of narcotics that as late as 1898 when heroin was introduced it was hailed as a sure cure for morphine addicts.
>
> In our attempt to amend the sanitation laws we were obliged to wage a bitter fight against the food lobby-the dairy industry, meat packers, the canners and preservers of foods. In our effort to prevent the unrestricted sale of morphine and opium we incurred the wrath of the drug industry by adopting resolutions notifying health officers to enforce the law. At first, our efforts were almost futile, but we began to learn a little about politics. In the San Joaquin and Sacramento Valleys and elsewhere, we formed associations of health officers to act with us as a unit in influencing legislators in favor of health legislation as well as improving standards of sanitation and health.

While Doctor Stansbury was struggling at the state level to improve health, others had campaigns in other areas. In 1875, and again in 1890, Bidwell was a third party candidate for governor, largely in order to publicize and promote the reform measures in which he believed. He was nominated in 1892 as the candidate for president of the United States for the Prohibition Party and received 264,000 votes. This was one of the strongest showings in history for a third party candidate. Bidwell was, and is, a folk hero, but he did not become President.

The 1870s big industry was lumber, either the milling of it or the shipping of it. Millwork began to be an enterprise in Chico. In 1883, the Stick-Eastlake style construction became popular. A house in this style, the Earll House, built at 238 Hazel Street, was completely milled in Chico, as were many others after that.

In 1871, the first few businesses began to receive gas lighting. In 1874, the Chico Gas Company brought primitive gas works from burning coal gas. The 1890s saw the real development of utility companies. The electric light bulb and the telephone were invented and put to use in this decade. In 1876, Chico had its first local telephone call. In 1889, the telephone line from Chico to Paradise was completed.

Natural gas was found and obtained in the Sutter Buttes and other places on the valley floor. In 1895, on a ranch 8 miles to the north, enough gas was found to light the town of Chico. Oil was seen floating on top of a mud stream on the site. On closer inspection, it was determined that natural gas was present.

CHICO

The local press revived sentiment for the "County of Chico" again in 1877. A petition was again placed before state legislature that was strongly opposed by Major Marion Biggs and George Gridley. Chico did not secede from Butte County, and this was celebrated in Oroville on the night of the legislature's decision. However, it was not celebrated in Chico. Citizens had filed a petition of 1,100 names requesting that Chico be named county seat.

In 1882, Chico gained access across the Sacramento River by the construction of a free bridge at Chico Landing. The cost was $27,000, and the northern end of the county contributed $10,000. It was destroyed in a flood in 1889. It was an expensive bridge and useful to the residents of the area, but it was only used for seven years.

John Bidwell subdivided the area north of his residence, called Chico Vecino, in 1889. The development extended from Rancheria Lane, now Sacramento Avenue, to the Lindo Channel. This subdivision developed slowly at first and then gained momentum.

The location of the Normal School Teachers' College in Chico was a consolation prize for the citizenry who had worked so hard on the county seat issue. Assemblyman Allen Henry offered a bill to the 1887 legislature to place a Normal School in the north part of the state. A group of 15 prominent citizens from Chico went to work to convince the legislators to choose Chico: William Earll, H.H. Camper, Allen Henry, C.C. Mason, Watson Chalmers, T.H. Barnard, A.L. Nichols, J.W.B. Montgomery, A.H. Crew, Charles Faulkner, L.H. McIntosh, F.C.Lusk, Z.W. Burnham, A.J. Bryan, John Bidwell, and G.W. Dorn.

The governor signed on the bill to locate the school in Chico on March 11, 1887. A committee came to look at the site. Bidwell was offering 10 acres, but the committee wasn't impressed with the location. He sent a telegraph stating, "You may take anything on my farm but my dooryard." They picked the present site on the south bank of the Big Chico Creek, fronting First Street. This was very close to General Bidwell's dooryard. Ten thousand dollars came from public subscription to defray the cost of building for the state. The committee received a telegram from committee member Z.W. Burnham, saying "Commence painting red. Chico has the unanimous vote of the Board. Burnham." Fifty thousand dollars was originally appropriated for the site, and later in 1889 the state gave another $40,000 to the project. Another $25,000 was given to finish, and the project was completed in September of 1889. The college opened for the 1889–1890 school year.

The first class of students numbered 70. Today the Normal School has expanded to become a California State University and enrolls 14,000 students yearly on a 117-acre campus. The area south of campus, where residences date back to the 1870s, has become almost exclusively student rental property. Over the years those older homes, many historic, have seen hard use and have suffered deterioration.

Athletics were organized for the school in the fall of 1895. The Chico State Normal School football team of 1902 had a six-game schedule. The team won all of its games for the season, with a total of only five points being scored against them. A typical cheer for the team at the time was:

> Rah . . . Rah . . . Rah; Wah . . . Who . . . Wah; Cal . . . iforn . . . ia; Ha . . . Ha . . . Ha;
> Chi-co Nor-mal; Zip . . . Boom . . . Bah!

The university grew in more ways than one. Student numbers rose from the first graduating class in 1891 of only 14 to a total of 939 students graduated in 1910; 450 of those students became teachers in the state of California. Annie Bidwell donated two more acres by the creek in 1910 to enlarge the campus.

Three literary societies at the university were the stimulus for public speaking, as well as social, literary, and musical interests. An annual debating contest took place with the San Jose school. *The Normal Record* was a school magazine, published four times a year, with a literary focus.

Changes were occurring rapidly all over town, and in the state, as railroads grew and business thrived. The Northern California Railroad Company wanted to tear down Chico's train depot and build a new one in 1892. The original facility had been built in 1869. It was shabby and inadequate. A separate baggage room was planned, as well as a ladies' waiting room.

Although the town was excited that a new depot would be built, and many had visions of becoming a resort-type area like Coronado in the San Diego area, the size of the new depot indicated that Chico would remain a smaller, rural town. The depot's most recent owner, the Southern Pacific Land Company, now leases the line from Union Pacific. Since Chico was designated as an Amtrak stop, the southern portion of the depot needed to be reopened as a waiting room. Research was done by the Chico Heritage Association to place the Chico Railroad Depot on the National Register of Historic Places. This qualified the site for a $60,000 California State Parks and Recreation grant. The City of Chico eventually purchased the building, and a modern-day fire destroyed the middle section of the structure. The renovation of the entire building, preserving its historical properties, was done in the late 1980s and into the early 1990s.

In 1901, the Diamond Match Company was planning its enterprise in the Chico and Stirling City areas. The plant located at the west end of 16th Street. The Chico Investment Company, largely made up of Diamond Match Executives, developed and sold off a number of subdivisions on the south side of town, which were quickly annexed by the city.

John Bidwell passed away in 1900, leaving Annie Bidwell with some debt to handle. She subdivided and sold many tracts of ranch land to settle debts and allow development in the town. The Humboldt addition may have been done by John Bidwell in 1900; however, between that time and 1908 there were at least 12 subdivisions created from Bidwell land and annexed to the City of Chico. One of these was the Lindo subdivision.

According to an article in the February 2, 2003 *Chico Enterprise Record*, J.J. Morehead built the Diamond Hotel, but it was probably his widow who supervised the project. The hotel was located on Fourth Street, between Salem and Broadway, in 1904. It was named after the Diamond Match Company. The hotel's opening was beautiful and luxurious. The food was exquisite, especially for the time. The article about the Diamond Hotel's refurbishing and re-opening in 2004 reported a surprising menu for the original opening in 1904: martini, oysters on the deep shell, caviar on toast, celery en branches, radishes, ripe olives, clear green turtle soup entasse, combination salad, laubenheimer, halibut au gratin, pommes nature, chicken patties a la reine, punch a la turque, roast wild duck, currant jelly, sparkling burgundy, cigarettes, hot asparagus, pommes au gratin, English plum pudding, hard and brandy sauce, Roquefort cheese, toasted cracker, assorted fruits, cordial, coffee noir. According to the 1904 proprietor, the hotel was "a first class hotel for first class custom."

There were those in town who did not think that the hotel had first class customs. When it closed, it was said to have had a "checkered career." George Robinson was said to have ridden into the hotel dining room on the Nichols Hardware delivery horse during one of the most elite parties of the year. A reverend of the First Methodist Episcopal Church, whose home was right next to the hotel, accused the establishment of running a house of ill repute. Some arrest records seem to indicate that there could have been something to the accusations; for instance, two men were arrested for giving girls liquor and keeping them in their rooms.

In 1916, the establishment became the Traveler's Hotel, a much less luxurious spot, which operated during the 1930s, 1940s, and 1950s. Its restaurant was a Hawaiian Café, and the cook was Joe Goon Fong, who was also the bartender. In the 1960s, the Traveler's Hotel was leased to the California State University and used as student housing. More recently, the hotel was used as a restaurant, first Mike and Eddie's and then Delancy's. Now the building is vacant and being remodeled as a hotel again. It will open as the Diamond Hotel in 2004, 100 years after the first grand opening.

Around the time of the Diamond Hotel, Chico crimes shifted to breaking and entering. Robbery was a favorite. Construction crews in the Oroville area were blamed but not necessarily guilty. The anger of the citizens grew and a burglar was shot and killed at a store in Durham in 1908.

The contest over the location of the county seat surfaced in the 1890s again. Chico citizens, not wanting to give up the fight, tried to form their own county, called Bidwell County. Chico citizens, of course, instigated the 1892 bill introduced in state assembly. Petitions circulated all over the west side of Butte County, but the bill was defeated by a vote of 37 to 33. Butte County was one of the 27 first counties in California and has been whittled down to its present size by annexations of neighboring counties—but not by Bidwell County, which was never to exist.

The Sperry Flour Company bought John Bidwell's mill business and built on the same site. Bidwell's mill had manufactured Extra Family and Golden Era brands of flour, graham flour, cornmeal, and stock feed. The new mill was a three-story structure run by water and steam power.

There was oil-drilling excitement in 1901 at the Richardson's Springs Ranch, outside of Chico to the northeast. However, there was not a sufficient quantity found to justify pumping. The Richardson brothers had built a hotel/resort area in the unique setting of their ranch. The Richardson Springs Hotel was a 14-room, wooden frame hotel completed in 1903. It advertised the healing powers of an old Indian spring, which claimed its waters had power to cure scrofula and other skin diseases. The mud from the springs soothed cuts, bruises, and wounds.

In 1921, the resort burned down. It was reconstructed and opened again in 1924. A second fire delayed the 1924 grand opening, but it was still a gala affair. The Richardsons were known for their hospitality. There were card games, movies, dancing, shuffleboard, swimming, hiking, tennis, and horseback riding, and a band was often on the dance floor on Saturday nights. People came from Los Angeles, San Francisco, and all over the valley to enjoy the resort and drink mineral water. The water sold as "Crazy Water Crystals" outside the area. This was the era of paregoric and other such exotic miracle cures.

There was a financial panic in 1907. Scrip was actually issued in Butte County. It was an unlikely time for development of an unconventional sort in the small town of Chico, but in spite of this a unique and mysterious venture began. The building is no longer standing but, apparently, it was exceptional when it was built. Annie Bidwell sold a piece of property for this venture to two gentlemen, Samuel R. Axtell and F.D. Robins, on March 3, 1908, for $1,200. It was located between Sierra Avenue (now East First Street) and the Big Chico Creek.

Often land donated or sold by the Bidwells included a stipulation that no intoxicating liquors could be sold or consumed on the property. This was the case with this lot. Additionally, Annie Bidwell hoped that this building would be especially edifying to the town. She hoped that organizations like the Young Men's Christian Association (YMCA) would be able to meet there free of charge. Following in her husband's tradition, although he had passed away, she sold the lot inexpensively for a good cause. The men intended to build an amusement place for a natatorium (swimming pool), skating rink, auditorium, ice plant, and cold storage plant, and because of the reduced price it was also agreed that the space could be used for the YMCA, the Union Evangelists, and other civic and Christian groups to meet without charge.

On August 11, 1908, the Rotunda Bath and Amusement Company was formed with J.W. Kerns, W.R. Brown, and B.S. Kerns as partners. The amazing, domed building was built with lumber from the Sierra Lumber Company flume and contained a natatorium in the basement, using water from the Big Chico Creek, a skating rink upstairs, a meeting room or auditorium, and an ice house. It was the place to go for swimming, skating, or to ride the merry-go-round. However, the edifice did not prove to be a financial success. In 1910, it defaulted on its note. Benjamin Kerns bought out the partners for a little over $5,000.

Chico historian, John Nopel, whose childhood home was only a few blocks from the Bidwell Mansion and the Rotunda, says he remembers seeing Annie Bidwell standing on her front lawn in the mornings, watching the construction or remodeling of the Rotunda building.

Later, the Brouillards, who ran the Rose City Wet Wash, a laundry business at the Rotunda, were asked to run the place. Mrs. Brouillard ran the swimming pool, which was used mostly by female customers. They held dances at the Rotunda, and they were lasting later and later. One night, when Mrs. Brouillard, who also lived in the building, was feeding the baby, someone threw a whiskey bottle down the chimney. The bottle hit and liquor went all over them. Mr. Brouillard ran up to catch the person. That was the end of the dances. Swimming was also halted abruptly when one day the dome crashed into the pool. Luckily, no one was swimming at the time. No one knows exactly when the pool was floored over, but it was soon after discovering the building was no longer safe. Records indicate that during World War II, the owners of the building lived out of town. These proprietors donated the building for use by teenagers. Young people cleaned the place, made curtains, and painted. They held dances and events there were chaperoned by Mrs. Philip Ware, Mrs. O.F. Gainer, and James Morehead. The building was razed sometime between 1951 and 1963.

The following is an ad for the Rotunda Bath and Amusement Company, reproduced in the January 1987 issue of *The Diggins*, a monthly publication from the Butte County Historical Society:

CHICO'S NEW AMUSEMENT ENTERPRISE
The Rotunda: The building in which is located a swimming tank 120 feet in diameter, holding 280,000 gallons of water; a scenic merry-go-round 70 feet in diameter, accommodating 200 people; an auditorium 126 feet in diameter, seating 4000 people. The building is located at the head of Flume Street, only two blocks from the main business section of the city, and one block from the Northern Electric Railway Depot. It is circular in shape and original in design and construction, having the largest dome in the United States.

Chapter Seven

CHICO GROWS

In 1911, a half-starved, disheveled, native Yahi Indian, who went by the name Ishi, wandered out of the foothills into the Oroville area. Speaking only his native dialect and terribly frightened of the townspeople, Ishi believed he would be killed when he entered town. He was bereaved from losing all his significant relatives and family, at a loss for his own survival, and felt it did not matter if he were killed. Ishi was determined to be from the southern Yana or northern Maidu region of California through an analysis of his dialect, but his remains have been returned to the Wintun tribe. Thought to be the last of the Mill Creek Indians, he expected to die, but instead was cared for, studied, and helped to continue his life among white people. This was especially so with anthropologists and language scholars, who tried to learn all they could about Ishi's way of life, traditions, beliefs, and general skills and knowledge pertaining to the environment of the native Yahi Indians. It was bizarre, and unfortunate, that the information would be passed on in this way, when once the area was populated with many native Yahi having this knowledge. So much had changed in 50 years. The world that Ishi entered into when he wandered out of the foothills had little resemblance to the foothills and valley he and his people had known.

The settlement of Chico and the Butte County area had not given a backward glance to the native life previously thriving in the area. Chico was battling fires, building up the city, conducting commerce, expanding, and improving. The same year that Ishi emerged, the old Chico High School burned down, and the new Chico Municipal building was built. A new high school was constructed at the present site of Chico High School, on the Esplanade on 50 acres purchased from the Bidwell estate.

The city of Chico Municipal Building was built at 435 Main Street, between Fourth and Fifth Streets, at a cost of $55,000. It still stands facing the city plaza. The federal post office was built on Fifth Street in 1916. Both the post office and the municipal building fronted the downtown plaza. Other stores in the area lost their old posts and wooden awnings, and the downtown area took on a "modern" look. Government architects, J.W. Roberts and Oscar Wenderoth, designed the buildings in a Renaissance Revival style.

Chico's Enloe Hospital got its start in 1913, between Third and Fourth Streets at 330 Flume Street, now the current location of the Women's Feminist Health Center. Newton Thomas Enloe, whose practice had started on the Paradise Ridge, had moved to Chico and begun practicing in the surrounding area. He opened the hospital that has served Chico for 90 years. A second building was opened in 1937, on the Esplanade, between Fifth and Sixth Avenues, where it is still located today. Ten new buildings have been constructed since that time to expand the hospital's services, making it one of Northern California's major medical centers. The delivery of the first baby in the new building occurred in 1937, a girl named Nansi Bohne. Sheriff Larry Gillick and his partner Russell Nothrup escorted her mother through a heavy snowstorm to the hospital facility.

Dr. Enloe ran the hospital until 1954. Then his son and two daughters (Thomas, Ida, and Nancy), became the administrators. Dr. Enloe's courage and progressive medical practices were a benefit for

Chico is known for stands of oak trees. These trees supported the local native tribe, the Mechoopda, with consistent crops of acorns. The Mechoopda cared for groves nearest their homes. They cleared beneath the trees to avoid fire danger, praying and dancing for rain to bring a good harvest. (Photo by D. Moon.)

The early natives in the Chico area were called "Kuksu" or "Big-Head Dancers" by the Maidu because of the headdresses they wore for ceremonial dances. (Photo courtesy of Michael Hicks.)

Steve Santos is the present-day Mechoopda Tribal Chairman. (Photo by D. Moon.)

This collection of native grinding stones was found at a Rancheria between the modern-day cities of Chico and Durham. (Courtesy of Chico Heritage Association Archives.)

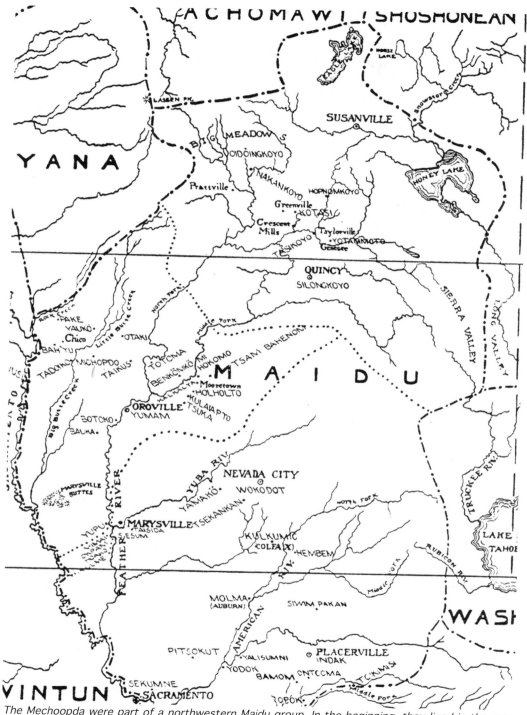

The Mechoopda were part of a northwestern Maidu group. In the beginning, they lived in the area of what is called Dayton today, to the east side of Little Chico Creek. (Courtesy of Mechoopda Tribal Library.)

The term "sweat houses" was used for homes that were for special ceremonies. (Courtesy of Meriam Library Special Collections.)

Some baskets, used as cradleboards, had sharp sticks attached to the bottom, for the purpose of staking the basket into the ground. The basket, containing the child, then could stand and allow the child to look around. (Photo courtesy of Michael Hicks.)

John Bidwell was born in New York in 1819. (Courtesy of Chico Heritage Association Archives.)

In 1847, John Bidwell managed experimental orchards and fields, flourmills, and fruit-drying operations on his ranch. This flourmill was built by the Sperry Flour Company on the site of John Bidwell's original mill. (Courtesy of Meriam Library Special Collections, John Nopel Collection.)

Settlers, discovering the beauty of the country and the vast food supply, began hunting and fishing in areas where the Mechoopda had once found their food. (Photo courtesy of Michael Hicks.)

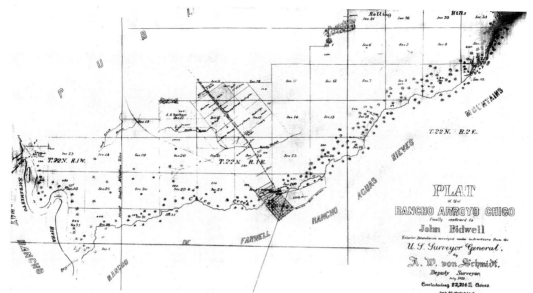

This old map of Rancho Chico dates from July 1859. (Courtesy of Meriam Library Special Collections.)

Dredging the rivers was one way of mining California's gold. (Photo courtesy of Michael Hicks.)

This Chinese procession through part of Chico's downtown is possibly a funeral procession. (Photo courtesy of Michael Hicks.)

The Chinese Dragon was seen in Chico over many years. The largest, most colorful dragon parade was at the New Year's celebration of 1900. (Photo courtesy of Michael Hicks.)

One thing was standing in the way of the development of California's agriculture—transportation to a broader market. (Photo courtesy of Michael Hicks.)

Chinese parade passing in front of Dr. Oscar Stansbury's home. (Photo courtesy of Michael Hicks.)

John Bidwell had a good rapport with the Mechoopda. He paid them in clothing and goods at first, then later with wages to work on his ranch. These Mechoopda children are wearing clothing of the times. (Courtesy of Meriam Library Special Collections.)

Annie K. Bidwell wanted all children to have the benefits of education and wholesome family life. Many of her gifts to Chico were motivated by these desires. (Photo courtesy of the Chico Heritage Association.)

A Mechoopda home sits on the Bidwell Ranch at the turn of the century at Rancho Chico. (Photo courtesy of Michael Hicks.)

At the United States Department of Agriculture Plant Introduction Gardens, plants from foreign lands were introduced to Chico farmers to see how well they could be grown locally. (Photo 1904, courtesy of the United States Forest Service Genetic Resource and Conservation Center.)

Rice harvests were common in Butte County in the early 1900s. (Photo courtesy of Michael Hicks.)

Almond orchards are a common, yet beautiful, sight in Chico today. (Photo by D. Moon.)

The Bidwells sit on the porch of their home. John and Annie Bidwell's correspondence was to last a lifetime, as he continued to write to her during their marriage. (Courtesy of Meriam Library Special Collections.)

A small Presbyterian church was built for the Mechoopda on the Bidwell Rancheria. (Courtesy of Chico Heritage Association Archives.)

The Mechoopda brass band was popular in town. They played on a number of special occasions and were well liked and requested by Chico residents in the 1880s. (Courtesy of Meriam Library Special Collections.)

Transportation at the turn of the twentieth century was still horse and buggy and an occasional bicycle. (Photo courtesy of Michael Hicks.)

The Engineering Department at the Diamond Match plant serviced locomotives and designed and manufactured logging "donkeys," or mechanized log pullers, like the one in this picture. (Courtesy of Meriam Library Special Collections, John Nopel Collection.)

The Dover *was a steamboat often seen on the Sacramento River, transporting people, wheat, hides, and construction material. (Courtesy of Meriam Library Special Collections.)*

The Diamond Match Barber Plant covered 125 acres and eventually developed a dozen buildings, including the Butte County Railroad Barber Depot. (Photo courtesy of Michael Hicks.)

Butte County Railroad "excursions" in the early 1900s were fun for everyone. (Courtesy of Chico Heritage Association Archives.)

The Dreiss Jewelry Store on Broadway was owned by Nellie Comstock and her husband, Charles Augusta Dreiss. (Courtesy of Chico Heritage Association Archives.)

This view shows the engineering building at the Barber Plant in Chico. (Courtesy of Chico Heritage Association Archives.)

Students pose in front of Chico's Sacramento Northern streetcar line. (Photo courtesy of Michael Hicks.)

The Southern Pacific Railroad Depot in Chico shines after its present day restoration. The first depot at this site at Fifth and Orange Streets was originally a California and Oregon Railroad Depot. C&O Railroad laid the original track through Chico in 1870. (Photo by D. Moon.)

The Sacramento Northern Railroad route led into the Bay area from Chico. (Courtesy of Chip Meriam.)

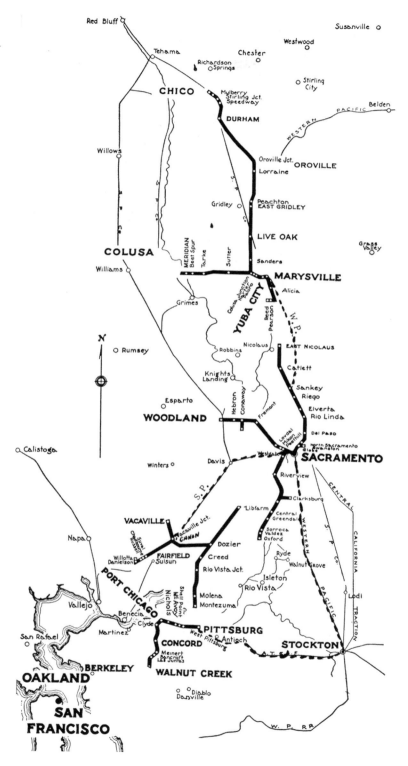

The first Western Pacific train leaves out of Oroville to Salt Lake City. (Courtesy of Matthew Livingston, family photo collection.)

This drawing is of the J.J. Morehead estate in Chico. Morehead was an early Chico area settler, banker, investor, and wheat farmer. (Courtesy of Meriam Library Special Collections.)

The Bidwell Mansion was a $60,000 project and was finished in May 1868. (Photo by D. Moon.)

In this photo of the La Grande Hotel, mud that plagued downtown Chico in winter is present. Diamond Match building crews finally constructed boardwalks to avoid this yearly problem. (Courtesy of Chico Heritage Association Archives.)

Every spring, the Bidwells' employees prepared an area of their ranch for public picnicking. Pictured here is a "children's picnic" in 1900. (Courtesy of Meriam Library Special Collections, Jon Nopel Collection.)

The Bidwell Building was originally a two-story structure, but eventually the top story was removed and two of the four walls were destroyed by fire. It was rebuilt, and the popular restaurant, Tres Hombres, retains one of the original walls and some original windows. (Photo by D. Moon.)

The Wright-Patrick Ranch House, now located on the Midway, was built by Thomas "Squire" Wright, Chico's first constable. (Courtesy of Chico Museum Association Archives.)

The triangular building on Oroville Avenue at the end of downtown has been a tavern in Chico since it was built (in 1865) until just a few years ago, with the exception of the Prohibition era. (Photo by D. Moon.)

At a Grange Hall meeting, Hester Patrick presides. Hester was active in civic organizations and historic preservation efforts. (Courtesy of Meriam Library Special Collections.)

The Chico Enterprise *was a stable competitor with the* Chico Record *for 75 years before the two papers merged to become the* Chico Enterprise Record. *(Photo courtesy of* Chico Enterprise Record.*)*

In 1877, the Chico Hooker Oak in Bidwell Park was the largest oak of its kind in the world. It was a California White Oak or Valley Oak, Quercus lobata. (Photo courtesy of Michael Hicks.)

Rains from the 1973 and 1974 winters were blamed for the demise of the great Hooker Oak tree in Bidwell Park. It lay in the park for a long while time before it was finally removed. (Photo courtesy of Michael Hicks.)

The Stansbury home is a credit to the community. The family members were the only owners and residents. In 1974, the home was purchased as a museum by the city of Chico. It has been placed on the National Register of Historic Homes and is preserved for visitors and the people of Chico to enjoy. (Photo by D. Moon.)

A two-story brick building for the new Normal School was started in September 1887 and completed in 1889. (Courtesy of Chico Heritage Association Archives.)

The magnum opus that housed the Rotunda Bath and Amusement Company was a round building called the Rotunda Building. (Courtesy of Chico Heritage Association Archives.)

Chico's Municipal Building at 435 Main Street still stands facing the city plaza. (Courtesy of Chico Heritage Association Archives.)

An arial photo shows Chico High School and vicinity. (Photo courtesy of Michael Hicks.)

The Chico Junior Art Club started the idea for Caper Acres, a fantasy-type playground for children in Bidwell Park. Barbara Hicks and Phyllis Wright, photographed at the playground site, were presenting the plans and drawings done by Marlys Norlie to the public. The development of Caper Acres was eventually taken over by the Chico 20-30 Club. (Photo courtesy of Michael Hicks.)

PRESENTED BY THE
MONDAY BRIDGE CLUB
1934

To show respect and gratitude for the enormous gift of Bidwell Park, the people of Chico wanted to make a special park entrance. A group of Annie's friends, the members of Annie's Monday Bridge Club, paid for the design and construction of the historic Park Entrance, at the corner of Fourth and Cypress Streets. (Photo by D. Moon.)

Under John Waterland's direction, swimming pools, using creek water, were built at One-Mile and Five-Mile. They were named for their distance from the beginning of the park. (Photo by D. Moon.)

This view shows the Five-Mile Dam in 1960. (Photo courtesy of the King family.)

Benjamin and Martha Kerns and their children before 1900. Thadeus, born in 1895, is on Martha's lap. From left to right are (front row) James Walter, Ruth, George, and Samuel, (middle row) Benjamin Sr., Beulah, Martha Everhart, and Thadeus, (back row) Edna, Benjamin Jr., and John. A deceased child not pictured was Amy. (Photo courtesy of the Kerns family.)

Chico Airport facilities opened in 1935. (Photo courtesy of Michael Hicks.)

The location of the Oaks Hotel was on a site where a cattle corral had been in the 1860s. It was a gathering place for Chicoans for 48 years. (Photo courtesy of Michael Hicks.)

The Chico Police force poses 1941–1942. Police Chief Charles Tovee stands in front; Bill Mathews, on the force at the time, stands next to him on the left. (Photo courtesy of Frances Mathews.)

The Chico Colts Baseball Team were the 1935 Champions. (Photo courtesy of Ann Sigel.)

The 1920 Chico High School Baseball Team is as follows: Venos Patterson, Blount (coach), Mitchell, Carmack, Mackay, Adams, Canfield, Brayton, Jones. (Courtesy of Chico Heritage Association Archives.)

Dave Sigel Sr. played first base for the Colts and was the owner of Sigel's Men's Clothing Store downtown. He also served as a City Council member and helped establish the freeway through town. The newspaper cut line for this picture was: "Dave Sigel classy fielding first sacker for the Colts who will appear against the Woodland Oaks here Sunday afternoon. Dave is showing improvement and ran wild on the base paths last Sunday evening at Grass Valley." (Photo courtesy of Ann Sigel.)

A May Day Celebration, started by the Bidwells in the park lands on their property, was the forerunner of the Pioneer Day Parade of Chico today. (Courtesy of Meriam Library Special Collections.)

Eugene Pallette pauses during the filming of Robin Hood *in Chico in 1937. (Photo courtesy of Frances Mathews.)*

Robin Hood (Errol Flynn) and stand-in for Maid Marian take a break. (Meriam Library Special Collections.)

The filming set for Robin Hood used most of the studio's Technicolor cameras. (Photo courtesy of Frances Mathews.)

Errol Flynn stars as Robin Hood. (Chico Heritage Association Archives.)

Olivia de Havilland and crew are interviewed at the Robin Hood filming site. (Courtesy of Chico Heritage Association Archives.)

The Senator Theatre stands as it once looked through the downtown plaza park trees, 1970. (Courtesy of Chico Heritage Association Archives.)

The tower of the Senator Theatre was removed due to deterioration. Funds are being raised to restore the building to its 1930s splendor. (Photo 2002 by D. Moon.)

The State College offered a variety of entertainment to Chico residents. This is an action shot of the University's 1940s basketball team. (Photo courtesy of Ann Sigel.)

The Honorable Theodore Meriam was mayor of the City of Chico from 1949 to 1959. (Photo courtesy of Chip Meriam.)

*This map of Chico was drawn in
1950. (Courtesy of Ann Sigel.)*

This drawing is from the Esplanade expansion plan of 1956. (Courtesy of Ann Sigel.)

The Oroville Dam and Sacramento River offered miles of shore line for recreation. (Photo courtesy of the King family.)

Two hunters display their deer. (Photo courtesy of Frances Mathews.)

Mary King sits with her proud catch of striped bass. (Photo courtesy of the King family.)

Bill Mathews was a pro wrestler from Chico 1935. (Photo courtesy of Frances Mathews.)

Chico Enterprise *editor Chet Dahl notifies Chico that World War I has ended. (Photo courtesy of the* Chico Enterprise Record.*)*

In Butte County, the railroad developed from the lumber industry's need to transport timber. (Courtesy of Meriam Library Special Collections.)

Orient and Flume, a local manufacturer of fine hand blown glass, is located in Chico on Park Avenue. (Photo by D. Moon.)

Chico State College became part of the State University system in 1972. (Photo by D. Moon.)

The university was in its third building phase in the 1970s. (Photo courtesy of Michael Hicks.)

Kiwi fields became a common sight in and around Chico from the 1960s through 1990s. (Photo courtesy of Chico Heritage Association Archives.)

The Nottleman building in the early 1900s. (Courtesy of Chico Heritage Association Archives.)

The threat of losing the Nottleman building, pictured here in 1969, helped raise heritage awareness. (Courtesy of Chico Heritage Association Archives.)

*This view
shows Main
Street looking
south, with the
Senator
Theatre tower
on the left, in
1969.
(Courtesy of
Chico Heritage
Association
Archives.)*

The Park Hotel on Fourth and Main Street is no longer standing. After losing some historic buildings and a few close calls on others, Chico residents began "realizing that history on local and state levels is just as important as national history." (Photo courtesy of Michael Hicks.)

This scene shows what one would see upon entering Chico in 1920–1930. (Courtesy of Chico Heritage Association.)

Chico said goodbye to electric streetcars in 1947. (Photo courtesy of John Nopel.)

News about historic buildings appears in the Chico Enterprise Record *and citizens have a growing awareness of Chico's past. (Photo courtesy of Ann and Tony Sands.)*

Corporate-owned businesses are a new sight in Chico. The presence of these corporations means that fewer Chico businesses are locally owned. (Photo by D. Moon.)

Oser's Department store on Third and Main Streets was locally owned. It was in business in Chico for 108 years. (This 1969 photo is courtesy of Chico Heritage Association Archives.)

The new mall in Chico is located on 20th Street in a large commercial redevelopment area. (Photo by D. Moon.)

Kou Lee, Rosedale School Hmong liaison in 1990, shows parents a video explaining the history of the Hmong in Laos. (Photo courtesy of Rosedale Elementary School.)

Families set up and do business selling flowers, garlic, onions, greens, strawberries, tomatoes, vegetables, and other high quality goods in Chico's outdoor markets. (Photo by D. Moon.)

Debra Moon instructs Hmong students in English Language Acquisition and Development, 1991. (Photo courtesy of Rosedale Elementary School.)

Mechoopda new tribal headquarters are located on Mission Ranch Road. (Photo 2002 by D. Moon.)

The new bike path for Chico residents follows the old train tracks. (Photo by D. Moon.)

In a protest held in the downtown plaza, Chico residents expressed their opposition to the War on Iraq, February 2003. (Photo by D. Moon.)

The Sierra Nevada Brewery started in 1980 and now employs 300 people in Chico. (Photo by D. Moon.)

Clifford's Jewelry Store (above and below) moved one block south from its original, early 1900s site. However, it has remained on Broadway in downtown Chico for almost 100 years. (Courtesy of Mike Hicks, owner of Clifford's Jewelry.)

The Chico Area Recreation District (CARD) Community building on Valombrosa is an unusual award-winning structure with well-planned construction and landscaping. (Photo by D. Moon.)

Chico's Downtown Business Association sponsors Thursday Night Markets and Friday Night Concerts downtown, which Chicoans of all ages enjoy. (Photo by D. Moon.)

Another walnut orchard was sacrificed to build Disco, a discount department store. When the store opened its doors, between 5,000 and 6,000 people shopped there during its opening hour. (Photo courtesy of Michael Hicks.)

Vintage Iron, a local Chico heritage group, harvests wheat at the Northgraves-Compton Ranch a few miles south of Chico for a Threshing Bee held in 2003. (Photo by D. Moon.)

the Chico community. Enloe Hospital was purchased by a group of residents, forming a non-profit company, in 1965.

In another county seat race in 1914, Chico lost the fight again. More citizens, with more energy than ever, enacted the rivalry for county seat between Chico and Oroville, but Chico was defeated. After a proposal by the County Board of Supervisors in 1914 to build a hall of records for county use, Chicoans once again became disgruntled about the location of the county seat. They circulated a petition to remove it from Oroville and place it in Chico. They gained enough signatures, all of which were carefully verified as signatures of previous voters. However, on voting day, the measure lost badly and the county seat remained in Oroville. This initiated serious consideration of county affairs. A committee was formed to write a charter for the county, which was finalized in 1918, ending with the acceptance of the Charter for Butte County Government. In celebration, the first Butte County Fair was held at the Esplanade, in Chico.

Other excitement in Chico included the filming of *Folly of a Life of Crime*, the first-known movie filming of many in town, in 1913. *The Diggins* describes *Folly of a Life of Crime* being shot at the church on Sixth and Flume and in Bidwell Park, near the golf course. Annie Bidwell granted special permission for the filming of this autobiographical story of Chris Evans and George and John Sontag, three of California's worst criminals. Vigilantes killed John, and Chris and George were sent to prison. Once they were released, the two surviving men decided to make, and star in, this film about their life of crime and reform.

Other movies that would be filmed in Chico included *Robin Hood*, *Gone With the Wind*, *Alamo Charlie*, *This Above All*, *Last of the Cowboys*, and *Kane*, among others. Some of the actors Chico remembers are Liz and Richard Burton, Olivia DeHavilland, Errol Flynn, Sidney Poitier, and Basil Rathbone.

Annie Bidwell had many good friends in town. The Monday Bridge Club was the source of some of her best friends, and another group she associated with was the Native Daughters of the Golden West. Annie was not born in the West, but the group honored her by naming the Chico Chapter after her. The first meeting of The Annie K. Bidwell Native Daughters of the Golden West, Parlor Number 168, was in 1908. Mrs. Bidwell donated a vacant lot to the parlor at First and Main Street, located at 50 Main Street. It had previously been used for cowboys to tether their horses while visiting downtown.

The Native Daughters met in several places: the Elks Hall on Second Street between Broadway and Salem, and the Independent Order of Odd Fellows Hall over Lee's Pharmacy on Broadway and Third. F.C. Lusk, a banker and highly respected member of the community, allowed the Native Daughters to meet in his home. The Lusk home, built in 1883, was purchased by the Parlor in 1933. They took on the project of beautifying Caper Acres in Bidwell Park for the enjoyment of the children in the community. They placed markers at several historic sites in the Chico area, and donated funds to preserve the Stansbury home and support the Chico Museum. They also participated in the Chico Southern Pacific Railroad Depot restoration.

The Masons and the Odd Fellows started out in the same building, the Collier's Hardware Building upper floor, for their meetings. The groups divided the space in half. Once the building on Broadway and Third Street was completed, the Odd Fellows met there in the upper story. The Elks met above The Majestic Theatre, which later became the El Rey Theatre, between Broadway and Salem on Second Street downtown.

CHICO

Economics remained grim in the country until the country's involvement in World War I. The outbreak of the war was in 1914. The United States, however, remained neutral. Effects of the war were felt in Chico, whose crop production had skyrocketed. An intensive chrome mining effort was undertaken locally as well. Food was produced and canned to feed the nation and the troops. The Americans became involved in the fighting and were involved until armistice, on November 11, 1918. During this time, 30,000 acres of rice were planted in Butte County, and the state of California started a state colony in Durham, south of Chico, to promote agricultural production.

It was earlier that year, on March 10, 1918, when Mrs. Annie Bidwell died. The park that Chico citizens had always enjoyed became the property of the city on the day she passed away. At the time Bidwell Park contained 2,250 acres of land, maintained with natural plant and animal life for the pleasure of the public. The park follows Big Chico Creek along the canyon for 10.5 miles.

The Bidwell Park and Playground Commission was created by John Waterland to oversee the park's maintenance. The park contained two swimming pools uniquely constructed to fit into the flow of the Big Chico Creek, picnic grounds, facilities, ball fields, playground, graveled and paved roads, municipal golf course, and a bandstand with seating. People have picnicked, played golf or ball games, and relaxed and enjoyed the scenery at the park for decades. It has been the site of Hollywood filming and is one of the ten largest parks in the nation. Its presence colors the life and times of Chico. "Shakespeare in the Park" is now performed annually in this idyllic setting.

To show respect and gratitude for this enormous gift, the people of Chico wanted to make a special park entrance. A group of Annie's friends, the members of Annie's Monday Bridge Club, paid for the design and construction of the historic Park Entrance at the corner of Fourth and Cypress Streets.

John Waterland, of the park commission, was a Chico pioneer and history student. Waterland graduated from Chico grammar schools in the early 1880s. He worked at the *Chico Record* for a number of years. He wrote the "old-Timer" series, which are popular today and have seen several reprints in the paper. Waterland volunteered six and a half years of daily attention to the improvement of Bidwell Park. Under his direction, the pools were built at One-Mile and Five-Mile. They were named for their distance from the beginning of the park. This space became an asset to the city by the time Waterland's term ended.

Benjamin Schuyster Kerns, another remarkable Chico citizen, was a Civil War veteran for the Union who came to Chico after the war. He married Martha Everhart, and they had 10 children. Ben Kerns became a successful businessman in Chico. He was the owner of the Rotunda building with its Bath and Amusement Company. He also participated in the movie entertainment business and other investments. He was a rancher and banker. He drained swampland and helped many of his children build on the drained land and produce crops. Their homes were north of town, near the current location of Shasta Avenue.

Ben Kerns, from Klamath Falls, Oregon, grandson of the original Benjamin Kerns from Chico, said:

> Dad (James Walter Kerns, Benjamin Schuyster Kerns' son) told me he once ran a film theater owned by his father. He told me he had silent movies, and some vaudeville. They tried sound movies with a phonograph alongside of the film [that way] Dad would try to keep the sound going with the talking people.

It was Benjamin's youngest son, Thadeus, who was a recognized child prodigy. In 1909, when Thadeus was 14, he began studying aviation. At age 16, he had built two gliders. He and his friends often soared off the cliffs around Chico, mounted on a glider. Thadeus was the first person in the county to build a motor-powered airplane. It was underpowered and barely made it off the ground. Not discouraged in the least, Thadeus built a bigger, better plane. Ben Kerns financed his son's project, which was a wood and canvas craft that Thadeus built at their family home on Shasta Avenue.

By the time Thadeus was 17, he was flying in circuits and at fairs. He was well known for his daredevil stunts and his flying skill. His adventures were carefully watched and covered by reporter D.W. Sutherland of the *Chico Enterprise*. Thadeus's family finally prevailed upon him, when he was 19, to give up this pursuit to get an education and take an interest in business. Thadeus had just returned from a successful circuit to Kansas when he confided to the family that he was convinced most pilots did die in crashes, so he would give up flying and take up the development of parts, particularly propellers, for the aeronautical industry. He couldn't resist a last flight in his aircraft, which had just been uncrated and assembled from the train upon arrival home from the circuit.

While the whole family stood outside and watched, he flew to the Sacramento River and then up to the foothills, all visible from the front porch of their home. He soared over the house and positioned the plane to land, when a spar snapped and one wing broke in half. The propeller, still turning, ripped through the canvas, and the plane screamed to the ground. Thadeus was killed and his family, who was close knit, was inconsolable. Dr. Enloe reported that Thadeus had broken every bone in his body. They burned the remains of the crash and moved away from Chico because looking out their dooryard made them too sad. Two of the boys, James Walter and John, with $10,000 each from their father, moved to Klamath Falls to start a utility company. Other members of the family may have moved there also.

Chico was the site of other aviation activity during the early 1920s. War ace Captain Eddie Rickenbacker came to the area to investigate the *Friesley Falcon*, which was transferred to a ranch between Gridley and Chico for completion of construction. The *Friesley Falcon* was a plane designed to carry 12 passengers or 3,000 pounds of cargo. This much needed, new development caused great excitement in the aircraft industry. The day the *Falcon* flew, 17,000 people assembled in Gridley to see its maiden voyage. Piloted by Rickenbacker, the plane cruised around Butte County and landed in Gridley, transporting several flight aces as passengers.

Pat Patrick established a flight school and a small airport on his property on the Midway in 1929. The first airplane arrival at the Chico Municipal Airport, very small at the time and located outside of town to the north, was on March 2, 1935.

In addition to airport facilities, Chico added five suburbs to the city and began planning the State Highway 99 East around 1918. The Oroville-Chico Road and Chico-Humboldt Road were both later incorporated into this appropriation.

The Hotel Oaks' formal opening was on December 12, 1918, with a grand banquet. Performing were singer Elmer La Fonso, a tenor, and the Majestic Orchestra, followed by dancing. The actual location of the hotel was on a spot where a cattle corral had been in the 1860s. The Hotel Oaks was a gathering place for Chicoans for 48 years. Robbins King, biology professor at the Chico State College in the 1950s, remembers stopping by there after work. This would have been convenient, since the hotel and bar were located across Second Street from the university. The Hotel Oaks was the site of city meetings, business negotiations, and community gala affairs. It was fun and beautiful, and a memorable place for Chico.

CHICO

A 1920 census for Chico showed a population of 15,517. Chico had grown more than expected, even through some rough times. The county's population at that time was 42.2 percent urban compared to 1910, when the population was 27.9 percent urban, and 1900 when it was only 15.4 percent urban.

During the latter part of 1921, the Progressive Club of Chico planned the planting of pistachio trees down the Midway after obtaining them from the Plant Introduction Gardens, with permission from Director J.E. Morrow. The Rotary Club organized everyone to come out on the morning of February 13, 1922 and help with the planting. Everyone was competing to have a hand in the project. By noon, 200 trees had been planted. Diamond Match declared a half-day holiday for any employees who wanted to participate. Twenty-five legionnaires showed up claiming they had been trench diggers in France and were ready to work. People now come from afar to photograph the scene down the Midway, where the two rows of trees gracefully touch the tips of their branches in an archway overhead.

The chamber of commerce wanted to plant elms for the remaining portion of the Midway to Durham. Also, a few of the pistachios had not survived and needed to be replaced, so, on February 13, 1923, another planting bee was organized. One hundred businessmen participated this time, and over 200 trees were planted that day as well.

A May Day Celebration, started by the Bidwells in the "park" lands on their property, was the forerunner of the Pioneer Day Parade of Chico that people know today. In May of 1915, senior students were invited to see the Normal School campus and were given a tour in hopes of enrolling them for the following year. The next year, on Senior Day, a parade was planned down Main Street, which still had two sets of tracks. It became tradition to have a big picnic, put on by the faculty, and a pageant called "El Progresso," depicting the progress of the community, staged on the banks of Chico Creek. There were 350 characters in the 1919 pageant. The celebration was held intermittently through the time of World War I.

In 1925, a western theme was started. A group of students and professors known as the Whiskerinos promoted the growth of beards, which were called "facial fungus" or "cactus crop." The Whiskerinos enacted a play about the Sheriff and little Nell (obviously, little Nell did not participate in the whisker contest). In 1929, the Grandfathers Club was appointed to preserve the ancient customs of these spring activities. The enactment of a skit called "little Nell and Sheriff" was developed as part of the doings. The longest parade Chico had ever seen occurred in 1931. It ended with an Old Timers Dance. Until 1932 Pioneer Day took place on a school day, when it was changed to Saturday. Gene Maxey and Betty Bonner raised interest when they met, as actors, in the skit of "little Nell and the Sheriff." Gene was a coach for the college. He later took little Nell (Betty) to dinner, and a year later they were married. This, of course, was reported in detail in the local newspaper, and everyone loved reading about it.

The 1920 *Chico High School Yearbook* was filled with Sherlock Holmes stories, puns and plays on words, gossip, smart remarks, and limericks. The *Normal Record*, a university magazine of the same period, contained much of the same fare: sequels and series, gossip and puns.

The first Homecoming Day for Chico State University was November 2, 1929, when 300 alumni returned. Miss Lillie Earl was the only representative of the original graduating class of 1891. The Laxon Auditorium at the college was added in 1931. Two years later, drama and music were added, and the Training School and Model Rural School was converted to a speech-music-science building. Aymer. J. Hamilton became president of the college in 1932. A celebration for Hamilton was held at the Laxson Auditorium. Plans for a new library were announced. It was to be called the LARC, or Learning Activities Resource Center.

The Bidwell Mansion was used as a girls' dormitory with strict rules for silence in study areas and meals at regular times. However, students were not able to meet the costs of living there during the Depression. A.J. Hamilton, university president during the Depression, announced that it would be given to the Home Economics department, where classes could be held and meals prepared for the students as a component of the classes. The first floor could still be used for student social activities. A number of old letters were discovered in the mansion at this time. They were taken to the main college building, where they were unfortunately lost in the fire of 1927.

The university generated entertainment and diversion in the community. Chico State was the host of an annual music event, the Northern Sacramento Valley Music Festival, where thousands of visitors flocked to the city for the occasion. Athletics brought more and more spectators. A popular man for many years was basketball coach Art Acker. The Wildcats captured the Far Western Championship in February 1937, and ever after coach Acker was known as the "Silver Fox."

The college was growing, and the city of Chico was having growing pains of its own. Chico was not finished with its scourge of fires, but the blazes became fewer and farther between due to improvements initiated by key citizens in town, not least among these Charles E. Tovee. Tovee was a stern character who emerged in Chico history around 1906 and influenced city life until 1953. In 1906, he joined the volunteer fire department. He was soon elected foreman of the Deluge Hose Company. He was the second assistant chief in 1910 and the first assistant chief in 1914. Tovee then became the city fire marshal and tax collector. Two years later, he was appointed fire chief of the entire city. Soon afterward, he became the city health officer and building inspector. He became the chief of police in 1923 and held the four jobs until 1947. In 1929, he became the chief of the city department of public safety. Then, in 1933, he headed the city's board of social services.

Sometimes Tovee would drive the water wagon. He was a little guy who wore cowboy boots. He was the fire chief, coroner, and police chief. He also owned a place of business called the "Duck Horn Saloon." Tovee retired as fire chief in 1953, and in appreciation for his contributions, Fire Station Number 2 was dedicated to him. One of his contributions to Chico was the development of the volunteer fire department into a highly trained group.

Charles Tovee was also ruthless in chasing crime and disease in Chico. As the Chinese population changed, and many family-oriented individuals returned to China, the concentration of opportunists in that part of town, especially old Chinatown, was high. There were some illegal activities, and Charles Tovee raided this section of town regularly. According to the *Enterprise Record*, bootlegging, smuggling, opium dealing, and gambling were frequent activities in the district. From 1916 to 1925, a man named Steven Ging was the reported crime lord of Old Chinatown. Ah Fong, Yen Ach, and Tong King were well known for gambling and opium dealing. Unsuccessful in his attempts to stamp out these crimes, Charles Tovee finally asked for help from federal narcotics officers to catch these characters in the act.

In 1925, Chinatown was proclaimed clean. It survived until September 4, 1944, when one of the worst fires in Chico history burned the entire district down. Only one building was left standing. It was commented that, "For years the lone two-story brick structure stood on the corner of an empty block like a tombstone."

CHICO

Tovee fought crime in unconventional ways. The following is a quote from the *Chico Enterprise*, referring to Tovee when he was chief of police:

> Addressing a modern day problem of low-life types riding around in cars in the downtown area in the evenings trying to convince young women to take "joy rides" with them, the Chief of Police Tovee solved the problem by having one of his officers dress up in feminine clothing and apprehend the men who harassed him. They were arrested immediately, taken into custody and given "floaters" out of town.

Joy rides were hopefully over, thanks to Chief Tovee and his officers, but Chico had other forms of entertainment. "The Chico Colts Baseball Team drew a big crowd every Sunday afternoon for years," according to Ann Sigel, wife of Dave Sigel, the Colts' Third Baseman. A baseball league formed in 1923, the Sacramento Valley League. Orland, Colusa, Woodland, Arbuckle, and Dunnigan were playing in the league when Chico and Marysville joined. Chico first appeared in 1925, but dropped out in 1932, then joined again in 1934. Two years before dropping out, in September 1930, the Chico Colts defeated the Marysville Giants for the Sacramento Valley baseball title. The Colts played every Sunday afternoon at the fairgrounds. They had some good players. Gordon Slade, a third baseman, later played with the St. Louis Cardinals and the Cincinnati Reds. George "Ice House" Wilson played for the Colts from 1937–1938 and then became the coach at Berkley High School.

The baseball program in 1940 took the team to task:

> The Colts have always been a team to pull out of the fire in the ninth inning. Why they wait until the last of the ninth we will never know. We have seen games where they have scored as high as five runs to win the contest by one run. From now on, we are asking them to play the ninth inning first.

Good semi-pro pitchers were hard to find in those days, which is probably why Larry Gillick, pitcher for the Colts, became so popular. He also recruited other good players and improved the team. He helped the guys on the squad find jobs in town so they could stay and play. Larry Gillick compiled the Colts' baseball programs, promoted the team, and kept it alive. Later Gillick became sheriff of Butte County.

Chico was a fun place. It had an ideal location for raising food and families. In the summers, families in Chico would load their kids into a wagon and take off for the mountains, for the day or a couple of days, to enjoy the cooler air. If someone moved away from Chico, they often moved back, as was the case with the Nopels. When the family moved back to Chico, they bought a grocery store. Nopel's Grocery, on the Esplanade, was near the present day location of Sounds by Dave. The Nopel's store had previously been Orendorff's. John Henry Nopel was congenial, and people liked him. The family lived in the building above the grocery store.

John Nopel Jr., local historian, grew up in Chico. In 1919, young John Nopel Jr. went to the Chico Vecino School, only one-and-a-half blocks away from where he lived. It was a two-story building, with grades first through sixth. There was no kindergarten then. He was a boy scout from the age of 12, starting in 1926. He was also active in the Chico chapter of Demolay, sponsored by the Masonic Lodge. The Depression had just started when John graduated from high school in 1931.

Chico Grows

Some of his friends were arranging to go away to school, but the largest percentage of his class was going to Chico State Teachers' College. John attended and graduated from Chico State with a teaching credential and was one of the fortunate few to get a job. He worked in Anderson, teaching a fifth/sixth combination class at a small school. He stayed three years but wanted to advance. In 1938, he went to Berkley.

John returned to Chico with a degree and a wife and family who agreed Chico was the place to raise children. John's involvement in the city life was complete. From the 1950s to the 1970s he was still involved with the Masonic Lodge and the Presbyterian church, and his three children attended schools in Chico. He was the principal of Hooker Oak School, and later served as assistant superintendent to Butte County Schools for 17 years. John has a collection of over 4,000 historical photographs on slides that he has obtained from friends in Chico over the years.

Life in Chico was intertwined in the growing years. People knew each other, worked for each other's families, went to school together, or somehow were part of each other's lives. No one in the city could escape the national dilemma of the stock market crash in 1929, and the ensuing Great Depression began a low point for Chico. The worst of the Depression was seen between 1932 and 1933. There were 500,000 unemployed in California in 1932. In 1933, Franklin Delano Roosevelt was elected president of the United States and the New Deal was cooked up immediately. It was welcomed and brought jobs through the Works Progress Administration (WPA), Public Works Administration (PWA), and the National Recovery Administration (NRA). In 1932, the total jobless in the nation totaled 6 million. A 100-day session of Congress forged the Emergency Banking Relief Act, Agricultural Adjustment Act, Federal Emergency Relief Act, the Civilian Conservation Corps, Civil Works Administration, Federal Bank Deposit Insurance, Commodity Credit Corporation, Tennessee Valley Authority, and more.

The university amphitheater on the north bank of Big Chico Creek was built with WPA funds. The city engineer, Frank Robinson, drew the plans. The federal government provided $3,403 and the WPA labor. The amphitheater is 80 feet by 40 feet, with a seating capacity of 750. Some of the work on the downtown Senator Theatre was also paid for with WPA funds. These federal projects eased the unemployment burden in Butte County.

The Depression and the New Deal renewed the need for agriculture business in the Chico area; agriculture was big, and it just kept growing. The almond crop in 1930 increased 26 percent. The Department of Agriculture was interested in enriching production and fostering more farming in America. Sugar beets were introduced into Butte County in Hamilton City. A sugar beet factory was built there in 1907 and the plant provided a cash crop to sell to the factory, as well as feed for stock. In 1908, William Grant (of the Department of Agriculture) wanted to research growing rice in America. A series of experiments were performed by a gentleman named Mackie, west of Biggs on land owned by the Balfour-Gutherie Company.

The Plant Introduction Gardens in Chico discovered the pistachio tree from China in 1914. The pistachio was tasty and took to California soil and climate extremely well, and sales of the food helped the Chico area. Farmers experimented with other crops also, and some produced and sold better than others. It was helpful to have the Introduction Gardens, with Director James Morrow and other experts close by, as farmers tried to find viable cash crops.

World War I was the impetus for intensive improvements in the agriculture industry in Chico and the exploitation of other natural resources. Needing to produce food for war-torn countries, such as France, and for U.S. troops overseas, the federal government encouraged the production of grains, produce, and canned foods. In 1918, the state embarked on the colonization of land near Durham for a national food production experimentation project. Dr. Elwood Mead purchased 6,300 acres of land with state funds. The state appropriated $260,000 for the project land purchase. $10,000 was for preliminary preparations of the land, and the remainder was for loans for land purchase and improvements.

The idea was to initiate more farming, resulting in more food production. Durham remained a state colony until 1935, when the project was liquidated and considered a failure. The farmers were never able to produce enough to repay the loans. However, the project allowed many small farmers to acquire land and produce crops. The Durham-Chico area continues to produce almonds, which was the subject of one of the main experiments of the project.

In 1942 Diamond Match started a tree farm near Chico, the second oldest in the nation. This 220,000-acre farm was the first established in California. This was an outgrowth of the effort started by the company in 1907, in which a forester was hired to establish scientific forest management, watershed conservation, a nursery for seedlings, fire protection, and disease control. Later, the Tree Farm and the Plant Introduction Gardens combined efforts to become the present day U.S. Forest Service Genetic Resource and Conservation Center in Chico.

As the area, and all of California, became more involved in agriculture as an industry and an economic base, water rights became crucial. The Western Canal Company was requiring their water users to buy stock in the company, an issue that went into litigation, with several reversals of decisions before resolving with the ruling that consumers were not obligated to buy stock. Over time, a new water doctrine was created. Nineteen-thirty-five saw 80 years of riparian water rights appropriated to a new set of rules. Underground regulation, floodwaters for flood control, irrigation, recreation, and power policies were introduced and upheld by a Supreme Court decision on January 31, 1935, and by the California State Constitutional Amendment of 1928. The Shasta and the Oroville Dams were built as a result of this new doctrine. The Central Valley Water Project impounded excess waters, underground waters, and storage waters for the above stated use as a public and private benefit.

The population of Butte County in 1930 was 34,093. By January of 1938, it was estimated to be over 40,000. It rose during the Depression, while elsewhere the population fell. In 1938, Butte County had 1,969 unemployed, and by 1939 the national unemployment rate was high at 14.5 percent. The merchants in Chico remained afloat but let many employees go. Bankers were hanging on to money. They were ordered to pay depositors a percentage of their claims. Chico printed its own currency to help families whose money was being held by one of two banks that were in trouble.

At this time, Othel A. Kilpatric, a member of the Chico City Council and mayor in 1933, opened the Kilpatric Markets. One of these he opened in the Bidwell building downtown, on the corner of First and Broadway Streets, which had become one-story by then. When Kilpatric opened "Kilpatric's Groceteria," it was the first self-serve, checkout counter–style grocery store in Chico, innovative at the time.

Although business was at an all-time low, three men applied for a broadcasting license in Chico in 1931: Harold Smithson, Willis Shields, and Sidney Lewis. In March of 1935, Smithson announced that the application had been approved for a 250-watt transmitter. The studio was nearing completion, and auditions were held daily to determine local talent. This was the beginning of Chico local radio station KHSL. Two years later, they received their license for 5,000 watts of power. In

Chico Grows

July of 1948, KHSL announced a new radio station, today known as KPAY, with 1,150 kilocycles and unlimited airtime, located on 230 acres of land outside of Chico, to the east on Paradise Road (now the Skyway).

A common crime in the 1920s and 1930s was violation of the 18th Amendment, the prohibition of sale or possession of alcohol. Crimes also included gambling, as well as other indiscretions. By far, the most bizarre crime during this era was the "turkey incident," reported at the H.W. Lewis ranch on Deer Creek. A ranch hand was working when apprehended by a woman, who sat on his chest and threatened him with her gun, while three other women selected and loaded up 100 turkeys. Since the ranch hand was embarrassed to disclose what had happened, no one knew until the turkeys were discovered missing. Neither the women nor the turkeys were ever caught.

The Depression brought Chico together. Although economics gave everyone a scare and some a set of hard knocks, fun was still sought. Many enjoyed the fame and excitement when Chico and other nearby sites were chosen by Hollywood for filmmaking projects. Chico's golden age of movies was from 1937 to 1947. Warner Street in Chico was named for Warner Brothers, during the filming of *Robin Hood* in 1937, which was probably the most popular and well-known movie filmed in Chico.

Before *Robin Hood* could be filmed in Chico several things happened. A Warner Brothers executive came to town and saw the enormous Bidwell Park. Richardson Springs remodeled and became the type of resort that stars could use as a getaway spot, and the Senator Theatre was built downtown in the late 1920s. The Chico Heritage Association Historic Resource Survey describes the building:

> It is an exotic Art Deco style building. The sides of the theatre are meso-american in inspiration, with stylized lotus flowers of an ancient Egyptian type. There are squat lions over the entrance. Inside, the design is Art Deco with floral and animal designs. The cost was $300,000, and boasted a Wurlitzer Organ, which alone cost $25,000. The architect was Miller & Pfleuger of the San Francisco Bay Area.

In the fall of 1937, Warner Brothers chose Bidwell Park as the site of the filming of *The Adventures of Robin Hood*. Director William Keighley stated, "There was no location in California that could compare with Bidwell Park." Errol Flynn, Olivia DeHavilland, Basil Rathbone, Alan Hale, and Patrick Knowles boarded a private train and made Chico their home for six weeks. They took an active part in the city's social life during their stay.

Errol Flynn played the part of Robin Hood, Allen Hale was Little John, and Olivia DeHavilland was Maid Marian. The movie was filmed in Technicolor, which was state of the art at the time. During the shoot, the *Robin Hood* crew used five of the eight Technicolor cameras Warner Brothers owned; each one weighed over 2,000 pounds. A lot of the weight was due to apparatus designed to mute the camera's noise as it rolled on the set and recorded the audio.

The filming of *Robin Hood* brought over 150 guests to Chico, who needed food, lodging, entertainment, and transportation for a long-term project. Actors and accompanying film crews took residence in or near Chico for the duration of the filming. This meant jobs in the off-season for many Chicoans. Local residents were also cast in bit parts. Jim Morehead documented the movie project by filming behind the scenes.

CHICO

Richardson Springs Resort employees knew all the stars on a first name basis. Filming of the movie concluded on November 8, 1937. This was over schedule due to rain and Errol Flynn dragging his feet. The film crew had to spray leaves in Bidwell Park with green paint, because by the final shootings for the film the leaves were turning autumn colors.

On May 15, 1938, crowds lined up outside the Senator Theatre to see the premiere of *Robin Hood*, and most people who saw it approved. The filming ran $750,000 over budget, totaling $2 million. During the three-day run, when the premiere was shown at the theatre, city schools closed to permit students to see a 2:30 p.m. matinee showing. Admission prices were $1.10 on the main floor, 83¢ and 55¢ in the balcony.

The Richardson Springs resort began to die in 1942, shortly after the filming of *Robin Hood*. The rationing of gasoline, food, and sugar put a damper on guest travel to the hotel. Soldiers stayed at the resort during World War II. In 1956, a renovation replaced the antiques with modern fixtures and furniture. A bar was installed, along with a recreation center for adults. However, Richardson Springs continued to lose popularity until 1968 when it was purchased by the Springs of Living Water, Incorporated, an interdenominational non-profit Christian group.

Shubert's, Chico's oldest and most-loved ice cream parlor, came to town during the same year *Robin Hood* was released as a feature film. Leonard Shubert, at age 54, came to Chico and was impressed with the tree-lined Esplanade Drive. He contacted H.K. Sears, a realtor, who introduced him to the Puritz family. He leased the building from the Puritz family at 178 E. Seventh Street, and it is still Shubert's present location. He opened for business on May 29, 1938, and in 1941 he hired his nephew, Charles Pulliam Sr., to help run it. When Shubert died in 1946, Pulliam continued to run the operation, eventually purchasing it from Leonard's widow in 1951. The back room was added in 1955, and in 1959 he added the candy portion of the store. Charles's four children worked in the shop as they attended college. A working partnership with Charles Sr., Charles Jr., and Glenn Pulliam formed in 1975. In 1980, Charles Sr. retired and sold his interest to his two sons. Now three generations of Pulliams work at Shubert's.

Chico was still a town where everyone knew each other. On June 11, 1941, the *Chico Enterprise* ran pictures of every high school graduate on pages four and five of the paper. Dairy delivery was advertised in the paper at that time. Grade "A" raw and pasteurized milk was available at the doorstep. The full price of a five-room home in Chico was $1,500, with $200 down. A ten-room home was available for $4,500, and a five-room house on Park Avenue could be rented for $14 per month. A 1940 Chevrolet Special Deluxe Sports Sedan cost $795. News in 1947 included reports on what ball players had the flu, and who had gotten traffic tickets. The news was nosy and gossipy.

Post-World War II days were different from days before it began. For one thing, Chico had a highly developed airport facility as a result of the Army Air Corps Training Center built there during the war. In August of 1941, Mayor E.L. Meyers received word that the Army Air Corps, as a training center, had selected the airport for air cadets. It was to be a $2 million station, with an annual payroll of $2.5 million, quite a boost for the city. The construction of 7,500-foot runways, a new road to the airport, modern lighting, a mess hall, and barracks were all part of the deal. Married cadets lived in Chico. The station hosted 1,900 men, including enlisted men and mechanics, who were quartered at the field. The Chico Army Airfield was activated on December 31, 1945.

Chico Grows

The City of Chico was the sole owner of the Chico Municipal Airport in June 1948. The War Assets Administration relinquished 34 buildings, a pumping plant, a sewage plant, and a railroad to the city, along with the airport.

The war brought other changes. The 1940s, in general, saw a shift and increase in population from rural to urban areas. The population of Chico in the 1940 census was 16,970. County probation officer, Lish Pool, made note of increased juvenile delinquency during the first two years of World War II. The rise was attributed to working mothers, lack of parental control, poverty, and unfit homes. In the spring of 1947, a 14-year-old boy in Chico murdered his friend, a 15-year-old girl. He seemed psychotic and had no motive for the murder. He was sent to the Mendocino State Hospital, where upon being evaluated as cured, he was sent to state prison. Japanese families were evacuated and taken to concentration camps. Later, this was seen as an unfair action caused by fears from the Pearl Harbor attack. After innocence of these families was realized, their needless suffering wrought national remorse.

In the last half of the 1940s, construction of needed projects were happening countywide. The mosquito abatement in 1948 was long overdue, as was the disbursement of Social Security benefits in 1947. Many new churches and schools were built, new radio stations, drive-in theaters, traffic lights, and parking meters (established in Chico in November of 1946). The city manager, Harry H. Hume, arranged the installation of parking meters in downtown Chico. He installed 600 at $80 each. A new bridge was built across the Sacramento River at Butte City. It was completed and dedicated in January 1949. In mid-May, a drive-in theater opened to a big crowd in Chico. Eventually, it expanded to accommodate 600 cars.

The headline of the Thursday evening newspaper of May 20, 1948, was "Tonight's Rodeo Cancelled, Wet Weather." It was the Chico paper's 80th year, and the paper price was 5¢ per copy or $1 per month. It consisted of 16 pages, which contained the following ads: Bravo Wine for 72¢, boy's jeans for $1.50 a pair, and Broadcloth sun suits for $2.98 each. The issue reported news on the school board, fraternities, the program for the fair, a story on a drunken driver, a battle overseas for Jerusalem, and a long story about spankings okayed by the school board for children who came to school with "ramps" on their breath. Apparently some students had been nibbling a powerful wild onion on the way to school that gave their breath an "odor like a polecat."

On October 2, 1950, Nichols Hardware, a favorite meeting place for ranchers and farmers for almost 100 years, and two other stores were lost to fire. Six fire units responded from 8:48 a.m. to 4:05 p.m. Nichols was located at Fourth and Broadway, where the Bank of America is today.

Ted Meriam was elected to the Chico City Council on April 18, 1947. In 1949, he was elected mayor. He served until 1957, the longest term yet in Chico. His father, Morrison Meriam, came to Chico in 1903 and taught at the Normal School. He married in 1905, sending for his sweetheart to come by train and join him. Anna Lund, his fiancée, was fond of Morrison, but not sure of her feelings about the West. She bought a two-way ticket in case she wanted to return after seeing Chico. Fortunately for Morrison, she never used the return portion of the ticket. The Meriam family still has that ticket and the purse she carried it in.

Ted Meriam was born in 1910 and grew up in Chico. He attended Chico High School and went to the Normal School, as did many other city youth. In 1934, he married Opal Meline, who also grew up in Chico. He attended the Normal School for two years and graduated with a degree in economics from Stanford in 1931. He wanted to continue with his graduate studies, but then the

Depression hit, and he was offered a good job at Oser's. His family urged him to take it and finish his studies later when money wasn't so tight.

Ted worked at Oser's part-time while he was a student at the Normal School and when he returned home for the holidays at Christmas. Helping out part-time at the store, he took over for an employee who was ill, performing a job of greater responsibility, at which time they offered him full-time employment. For Ted, Oser's became his lifetime employment. He worked his way into a management position, and then became part owner before the store closed in the 1980s. Several years after his wife Opal died, Ted married his longtime friend and co-worker, Doris Sherman McLean.

Ted Meriam made the first dial-up phone call from Chico. He called his daughter, Betsy. He watched the growth and development of the town and in 1949 became involved by running for city council. He remembered things such as wooden board sidewalks and fires downtown. During his last term, the first woman to serve on the city council was elected, Judy B. Conley. She became the vice mayor and was the only woman on the city council until 1973 when Elizabeth Smith was elected. Under Ted Meriam's leadership, the proposed Esplanade expansion plan was carried out, the freeway was built, the university grew, and the municipal airport became an industrial area with 100 businesses employing the residents of Chico.

No matter how careful the leadership was, continuous growth of the city finally presented preservation-related problems: the threat of demolition and inappropriate remodeling. Some incompatible additions were made to areas of historic concentration. Although the Chico Heritage Association historic building survey states, "The best examples of 19th and early 20th Century commercial architecture in the downtown area [of Chico] were emasculated during the flurry of the 1950s remodeling, influenced by the square-edged detailless International Style," the emasculation truly started before the 1950s, and Chico began to take on a different, leaner look.

After World War II, the native Mechoopda were still recognized as a tribe by the federal government, and they had their land in trust. They were living on a Rancheria near Mechoopda Avenue, in their third location since the arrival of John Bidwell. It was the same land that had been given to them by Annie Bidwell. Urbanization was surrounding them. They had not developed their housing and did not have the infrastructure the town had by the end of the 1940s. However, they were a strong group and a part of the greater Chico community. Yet harder times were about to descend on the Mechoopda, because the federal government ceased to recognize them as a tribe in 1958. Their land was deeded to them and they owed taxes that they were not able to pay. They became a "scattered community," struggling to hold together their traditions and lifelong relationships.

Chapter Eight

ENRICHING THE CITY

In February of 1950, 23,000 copies of a booklet titled "Surviving under Atomic Attack" were distributed in Butte County. North Korea invaded South Korea, and President Truman ordered troops in. That same year, several hundred Solano County residents evacuated to Chico during "Operation Chico" in an effort to escape what they felt was imminent atomic war.

The Oroville Dam, 27 miles from Chico, was built as protesting students and youth demonstrated unrest with the nation's policies in the 1960s. As the final height of 770 feet was reached at the Oroville Dam project, President Kennedy was assassinated, race riots broke out in many northern cities, and large anti-war demonstrations developed after Lyndon Johnson announced his intentions to triple forces in Vietnam. In 1966, the first young man from Chico was killed in the Vietnam War.

While the county generally remained more agrarian, the city of Chico was urbanizing rapidly. Between 1950 and 1980, the city underwent many modernizations and additions. The Esplanade was made into a four-lane highway, and Highway 32 was realigned from Chico to the adjoining Deer Creek Road. In April 1952, the Federal Communications Commission granted an authorization to TV station Channel 12 in Chico. Radio station KXOC secured a new dial position, 1060 AM, and a new power allowance of 10,000 watts. It was then designated as KPAY and has been serving Chico ever since. KHSL also began in the 1950s.

Early in the era, Purity Stores, Incorporated built a supermarket at the corner of Mangrove and Palmetto that cost more than half a million dollars. When Purity Stores opened their 100th market in Chico, popular Vice Mayor Judy Conley cut the ribbon for the 14,000 square foot building. In 1960, the new Mangrove Avenue Shopping Center took out an entire walnut orchard. A $5 million shopping center, later known as North Valley Shopping Center and Mall, was announced in January 1960 at East and Cohasset. Several downtown businesses moved to the mall, initiating urban sprawl in Chico. Montgomery Wards opened a $1 million store in Chico's North Valley Plaza.

In order to compete, downtown stores offered big sales and discounts. According to a report from a security guard, in those days when Oser's downtown department store had 6 a.m. sales, the police had to come. People lined up and mobbed the store as soon as it opened. Apparently, sales and discounts guaranteed popularity in Chico. A $2 million discount department store, called Disco, opened in Chico in 1965. Another walnut orchard was sacrificed. When the store opened its doors, between 5,000 and 6,000 people shopped there during its opening hour.

PG&E electric lines expanded in the 1960s. Lines and towers were built from Gridley, Table Moutain, Butte Meadows, Jonesville, and Biggs. In the early 1960s, higher wattage generators were installed to meet the area's growing needs. On September 16, 1960, the *Chico Enterprise Record* printed its 100th anniversary issue. It was the single largest issue of the Chico newspaper printed in the North Valley area. The 1965 Silver Dollar Fairgrounds attendance was a record breaking 64,384 people.

In 1964, Louis Olker founded Chico's second hospital. Chico Community Hospital was built on Cohasset Road, a central location for the city by then. In the 1980s, a Rehabilitation Center for burn and stroke victims opened. Community Hospital provided Chico more than 30 years of excellent community service when Enloe took over their facilities and expanded their services to the center.

While Chico mainstream business prospered, the Mechoopda Tribe suffered setbacks. They continued to live on the Rancheria near the Bidwell Mansion. Their first elected leader was Elmer LaFons, who was also leader in 1958 when the federal government declared they would no longer recognize the Mechoopda as a tribe. They could no longer afford to live on their land. One young Mechoopda woman paid her taxes and kept her land. All others lost their land or sold it, either because they could not afford to pay taxes and bring housing up to code or someone paid their past due taxes and took the land from them. Some went to live with relatives or other tribes, some moved to Grindstone or Clear Lake, and some stayed in or around Chico. Steve Santos said:

> The Mechoopda still came together for weddings, funerals, feasts and other gatherings. We gathered in each other's homes, had pot lucks. We were organized, and we had a group mentality, but no homeland. During 4th of July celebrations, and those types of things in Chico, we still took part. There was a time of reviving the dances, and especially the "Big Time" Celebration.

When Fred Davis became the director of public works, the population of Chico was only 13,000 and there were only 1,500 students at the university. The town's infrastructure was in bad condition. Chico was behind in development in the early 1950s and Fred commented:

> The euphemistic term was deferred maintenance, but what had really happened, was the Depression and the war had left many towns and cities without resources or materials to establish or maintain infrastructure. You just couldn't get materials, and small towns were really suffering. . . . Another problem was the unincorporated areas in the city. A 1960s city council resolved to get the needed revenue to fix the city up one way or another. A citizens' committee formed and passed some general obligation bonds. With that money we rebuilt the airport, put in some sewer interceptor systems [and other improvements]. . . . We went to the voters to increase taxes many times, and they never turned us down.

In the 1950s, construction of the freeway through town split city alliances. The council got 8,000 postcards from citizens expressing their opinions on the proposed route. Trucks and trains were traveling through town, and everyone knew that a freeway was needed. Wealthy and established residents proposed one outside of town, down Forrest Avenue. However, the rest of the population felt no one wanted to go there. The freeway had to go through town, and the path was through the homes of some prominent citizens. Fred Davis said, "It caused some hard feelings that lasted many years. People quit patronizing each other's businesses in town. They operated their own boycott. There was a well-financed opposition to the city council's plan."

Due to this controversy, a freeway agreement was finally made in which the state offered to do the landscaping. The council chambers were consistently packed during the debate. The editor of the *Enterprise Record*, Bill Bramwell, supported the council plan. The City of Chico held a trust with the parkland, and the state had to pay a price for an easement through it. Those funds were used to upgrade and improve the park, in general, for the city. The state even agreed to "fix up the Esplanade as part of the deal."

Enriching the City

In 1956, the day came for city council to vote on the freeway route. The council chambers were absolutely packed. The council members stood up and said they realized there was great opposition to their plan, but that the only recourse citizens had was to recall them. They agreed that if any one of them were recalled, they would all be recalled. They were standing together. Then they laid out their decision.

The opposition lost, and the result of the council's plan was a freeway system that is almost invisible. Driving through Chico on the freeway is almost like driving through a parkway. The exits are convenient to downtown, the university, and other development areas. The freeway is well placed and has served the community adequately for over 40 years.

Five new bridges were built in Chico. In September 1961, the Bruce Street Bridge for Little Chico Creek was completed. Two other bridges across Little Chico Creek were also under construction at the Pine-Cypress Mulberry Street complex. A new bridge across Lindo Channel was approved by city council in 1964 for the Longfellow area, which was completed in the fall of 1965, along with the opening of Pleasant Valley High School.

Chico levied taxes for everything. There was an airport tax, a tree tax, a school tax, etc. Proposition 13 in California eliminated flexibility in taxes throughout the state. It reduced property tax by about 60 percent in the early 1980s when voters passed it, but it made funds for special issues in the city harder to obtain. Chico had good city management and devised a plan to recoup their loss in tax money by charging development fees and annexing tracts of land that were soon to be developed.

One of the issues that came up during Fred Davis's 33 years as city manager was the fluoridation of water. He explained:

> That packed the council chambers many times, mostly with people who were against it. Eventually what happened was we determined it was just not cost effective to treat youngsters' teeth that way. It was cheaper to give them a pill. This also protected those who didn't want their children having it. We gave away big bottles of those pills to those who couldn't afford it.

The city of Chico is organized under a charter, a set of organized laws that are approved by voters in the community. The first charter for Chico was implemented in 1921. It was revised in 1960, and accepted by voters in 1961. When Chico started their charter, it was an advantage, but now the state has adopted many of the common charter stipulations and laws. However, Chico's charter provided stability to the operations of the town in the earlier years.

During the 1960s, a group of Chico residents, called the April Committee, tried to change the form of city government from the charter to the strong mayor mode. They did not succeed, but they did manage to elect a group of academically-oriented people to the city council, where before most council members were business people. In the late 1970s and the 1980s, another group in town elected an anti-development or anti-construction majority. This city council elected Mardi Worley, a woman, as their mayor in 1981. They were relatively liberal. This was a post-Vietnam era; some civic actions were motivated by anti-war sentiment. These council members were interested in helping low income families and protecting the environment. The leaders were David Guzzetti, Karl Ory, Bill Brashears, and others. They raised fees, supported a strong "greenline" to stop developers, and declared Chico a "Nuclear Free Zone" in a 4–3 vote.

In 1973, Butte Creek Canyon and the Chico foothills became a matter of public attention. A planned area cluster development in the canyon was rejected in a countywide election in 1981. There were over 19,000 votes cast against development and only 9,000 in favor. Later, development of the foothills was defeated by a group called, "Friends of the Foothills," led by Kelly Meagher, Mike McGinnis, and David Guzzetti.

Chico won awards for its fire and police service, which had improved and become sophisticated. Although their response to fire had become more precise, some fires were hard to prevent or control. In 1950, a fire on Fourth Street and Broadway destroyed $300,000 worth of property. At that time, it was the worst fire in Chico history.

Elmer Brouliard became the fire chief in 1956. The fire department held 90 school fire drills, showed 11 fire prevention films, and made more than 500 inspections and investigations. A new fire station was built on the corner of Ninth Street and Salem. It was an excellent location for fire service with its big yard for drills and training. Chief Brouliard was personable and received notice for greatly improving Chico's fire service. It was now a 21-man department, but it could not circumvent an even greater tragedy that occurred on February 2, 1970.

A fire, which started in and destroyed the Silver Room, a downtown bar between Third and Fourth Streets on the east side of Broadway, also damaged Sigel's Men's Wear. The greatest loss in that fire, however, was Chico's beloved fire marshall, Ray Head. His passing was much mourned in Chico. His wife was Helen Bell, of the Bell family, early settlers with a ranch north of town. Helen is still living. She and her sister Claudine are known as "C & H, the sweet sisters," named for sugar, according to Ann Sands, a living relative of the Comstock and Dreiss families, who were brought to Chico by Diamond Match.

The Chico Police Department claimed an "enviable record in prevention and suppression of crime." Chico's policy was to "hire capable men of integrity and to maintain a constant training program." In 1956 and 1957, Chico received one of six awards given by the National Association of Chiefs of Police for traffic supervision.

Although the city was a relatively safe place and crime was low, it steadily increased in the post–World War II era in Chico, as was the case throughout the nation. In February 1955, $165,000 worth of jewelry was stolen from The Time Shop during broad daylight.

In 1958, the community was horrified when a college freshman butchered a Chico woman in her trailer home with a knife from her own kitchen. Both the woman and the student were very drunk. In 1962, the number of forgery cases had almost doubled since 1957. Countywide drug arrests in 1969 were significantly higher than ever, and a juvenile hall school was started for offenders in 1972. Crimes increased in frequency and severity, and in 1979 ten murders were reported in the county in one year.

The population growth in Chico warranted the opening of a second junior high school and high school in the mid-1960s. Bidwell Junior High construction began in 1963, and Pleasant Valley High began in 1964. The Chapmantown Neighborhood Center was built in 1969 at 775 E. 16th Street. It remains a benefit to the neighborhood today, providing the residents with sports and community activities that assist children and adults to be healthy and involved with their neighborhood.

In 1875, the first free library and reading room opened in the old Bidwell Building at First Street and Broadway. Subscribers paid dues to withdraw books. In 1904, when Andrew Carnegie was building libraries throughout the country, Chico applied for $10,000. In order to get the money, cities had to own a site and agree to support the library. Construction of the new Chico Library started in the fall of 1904, across from the Lusk building on Second Street, and was ready for occupancy the next spring. Several years prior to 1945, the building became too crowded and a new wing was added for a children's reading room. Now this building is the Chico Museum, and the present-day library is on First Avenue and Sherman in a larger, modern building. In the 1960s, the city and county library services merged to conserve resources and provide better service to the public.

Enriching the City

Building improvements were not the only developments in a growing city. Life was becoming richer in many ways. The first Wildlife Refuge was established in the Sacramento Valley in 1931. The Gray Lodge Gun Club outside of Gridley was purchased by the State for $51 per acre. Between 1931 and 1952, more land was acquired until the acreage equaled 6,700 by late 1955. In 1970, the Marion Baldy property was acquired, adding 760 more acres to the south of the wildlife preserve. A new drainage system was built, making water supply and drainage less costly. During the 1950s, the increase in rice land in the valley created concern in farmers over the number of waterfowl eating their crops. In turn, the Gray Lodge Wildlife Area began cultivating food crops for the waterfowl.

The state also began regulating hunting of waterfowl in the area. Chico had become a popular spot for hunting and fishing and other family recreation. By 1980, only 2,400 acres were designated as a refuge for wildlife, and the remainder was set aside for regulated hunting. Studies of aquatic marsh plants were conducted on the refuge beginning in the late 1950s. Gray Lodge was one of the key bird-banding areas in the nation. The Sacramento Valley Waterfowl Advisory Committee was established in 1952 to oversee public hunting and general management of the refuge and similar areas.

An irrigation system was developed, and Gray Lodge became one of the most highly developed wildlife areas in the nation. Numerous field research studies have occurred there since 1952. Birds of the chaparral and birds of prey also found protection at the refuge.

The river valley contained a great variety of birds. There were band-tailed pigeon, mourning doves, quail, Sierra grouse, turkey vulture, chicken hawk, sparrow hawk, red-tailed hawk, march hawk, barn owls, burrowing owls, and horned owls of several varieties. California acorn woodpeckers, other varieties of woodpeckers, red-breasted sapsuckers, and red-shafted flickers also made their homes there. Along the streams yellow-bodied cuckoos, yellow-billed magpie, black phoebe, barn swallow, bullock orioles, brewer blackbirds, and redwing blackbirds could be found. Also seen were the much-disliked California jays, stellar jays, and American crows.

In May 1952, the county board of supervisors approved a master plan for the development of recreation areas in the county. Hunting, fishing, and love of the outdoors drew people of all ages to Chico. Riding and hiking trails were built in Bidwell Park and around Lake Oroville. Trout and striped bass drew the fishermen. Silver king salmon, steelhead, rainbow, white sturgeon, and Sacramento perch were also caught. Fish and Game later introduced brook trout, shad, and mosquito fish. Pheasant and duck hunting were popular in the valley and the marshlands. Hunters roamed the foothills for deer and even bears.

In his book, *Sabertooth: The Rip-Roaring Tales of a Legendary Game Warden*, Terry Hodges relates some unique hunting and fishing stories he experienced with his co-worker and game warden Gene Mercer. Mercer was well known in the Chico area and served as a game warden for over 55 years. It was not unusual for him to purchase fishing licenses for poor or hungry miners from his own pocket, rather than arrest them for not having one. A unique story that Mercer related to Hodges about an illegal deer hunting misadventure ended in a car chase with a woman standing on the running board of the get-away car and clinging to the car as it careened around mountain curves. Mercer saw the car disappearing ahead of him with the woman on the floorboard hanging on for dear life. He pursued them and discovered the man was a doctor in Reno, and that his gun, and the woman, belonged to another man. The doctor had bought the deer from poachers and was so badly shaken by the whole experience that he actually sold his practice and moved back to Ohio.

A person who lived the Chico life fully was pro wrestler Bill Mathews. Bill was a well-liked person and often went hunting with friends. He knew Gene Mercer, as most hunters did. Once, on a hunting trip, Bill shot a deer early in the day. Although Bill hid the deer well under the bushes while he went to do some fishing, when he got back to the camp, he discovered that Mercer had been by, found the hidden deer, and had already tagged it. Mercer had an uncanny sense that baffled hunters and stymied would-be poachers.

Frances Mathews, Bill's wife, related many fun hunting trips that she had gone on with Bill, but said that in the 1980s, once pot growers got started planting up in the hills, the whole atmosphere of hunting changed. There were barbed-wire fences where there had been none before, and men with shotguns. "It just wasn't fun, so we stopped going [to the foothills]."

Bill Mathews was the fastest man on his feet anybody in Chico had seen. He was a professional wrestler and boxer and on the bowling team as well. He often helped the instructor at Chico High School with the kids on the wrestling team. When he gave up his professional wrestling career, he gave his gloves to the high school. When Mathews moved to Chico his first job, besides wrestling, was as a lifeguard at Bidwell Park 1-mile area. Mathews also drove a water wagon when *Robin Hood* was filmed and was a bouncer who kept unwanted members of the public out during filming. He got acquainted with the actors, especially the stand-in for Olivia DeHavilland, Dorothy O'Connor. A couple of Mathews's friends were able to get bit parts in the film. When other movies came to town they tried out and got parts, too. Mathews joined them in *Stand up and Fight*, and in the movie *Big Little Town*, Mathews's car got the bit part because it had a dent in the fender.

Bill served as a policeman for the city for seven years. He also did delivery for Charles Pulliam at Schubert's for a short time. These men bought three acres together bordering Diamond Match land. Bill worked full-time on the Chico police force in the 1940s, when Chief Tovee was in charge, and helped him with all his schemes to fight crime. Bill did not escape being written up in the Chico newspaper, many times for his bowling and wrestling successes, and once for losing a box of shells in a bet. Vita Sheppard, *Chico Enterprise Record* columnist, wrote a popular gossip column in the 1960s and 1970s, and almost everyone's name appeared in the paper at some point.

As the city grew, so did the news as two new publications started in Chico. The *Chico News and Review*, a weekly newspaper that published its first issue in August of 1977, still publishes weekly. The original staff members were writers for the university newspaper and the publication had a younger, radical view on Chico issues. The *News and Review* tended to support protecting the environment, rather than needs of business people or developers. The *Chico Times*, also a weekly, was started in 1980 by an opportunist who later turned the paper into a coupon book. The *Chico Times* was created with a goal to bridge the gap between the more conservative Chico *Enterprise Record* and the more liberal *Chico News and Review*. The paper's slogan was "Both Sides Now," and often people with opposing views on Chico's issues were interviewed and both responses printed side by side on the *Chico Times* front page. After three years, the *Chico Times* folded and the *Chico Enterprise Record* continued to be the largest newspaper in the Great Mid-Valley area.

The Chico Airport industrial area was developed and approximately 100 businesses were established. The industrial complex had 200 acres of choice sites for general industry, and 200 acres available for aviation industry. There was unlimited water and electrical supply, as well as an excellent sewage disposal service. There were 6.5 miles of paved, heavy-duty streets with good drainage in all areas. The industrial park was a development of the City of Chico and the Western Pacific Railway. It was actually served by the Sacramento Northern Railway, a subsidiary of Western Pacific Railway.

The Mitchell Avionics Corporation was located at the airport municipal building with 92 employees. The other portion of the military project created approximately 150 jobs for people in Chico in the 1950s, mainly in performing maintenance and repair work for the air force and commercial airlines. The air force built a 1,500 by 3,000 foot, paved landing mat at the Chico Airport, which was then 1,055 acres.

Enriching the City

When the U.S. Army Air Force 452nd Command turned the airport over to Chico, it was the largest municipally owned airport in California north of San Francisco. Passenger travel and airfreight traffic have increased yearly. Now over 1,000 residents are employed at the complex, receiving a payroll of $3 million annually.

In 1960, an American U-2 plane was shot down over Soviet territory. The pilot, Francis Gary Powers, was exchanged for Rudolf Abel, a Soviet spy, in 1962. This, and other factors, led to the opening of a Titan Missile base north of Chico, which became operational in 1961. Test flights at Cape Canaveral proved that the Titan Missiles could carry a nuclear warhead at least 5,000 miles. Each of the three Titan bases contained three missiles, which were housed underground and could be launched at command in 30 minutes. In May 1962, an explosion and fire occurred at the Chico Missile Base, ruining one silo. The three bases were ordered closed on May 31, 1965 because they were obsolete. With the closing of the base, Chico lost 756 military personnel and 27 civilians associated with maintenance and operation of the missiles.

The missile base was abandoned and reconstruction of the Chico Airport began in 1969. People who were in high school at this time recall going out to the vacant silos, exploring them, and doing daring tricks. It was ironic that groups of people had moved to Chico to be free of nuclear threat, when one of three major missile bases were opened just 4 miles from town. Once the missiles were outdated, Chico received $309,203 from the Federal Aviation Administration to reconstruct the Chico Municipal Airport. The money was used as part of a proposed $800,000 project to build a new terminal building, runway, and taxiway.

A highly unusual business born in Chico, and located on Meyers Street in the south part of town, was the manufacture of the amphibious vehicle called the Coot. This is also the name of a common waterfowl, found in and around the Chico area, that cannot fly well and lives mostly on the water. The Coots were designed and developed by Carl Enos Jr. and weighed 750 pounds each. These vehicles could pass over heavy boulders or serve as a motorboat in the water. The assembly line production began in Chico in July 1967. Chico observed Coot Days starting in July of 1968. When the 1,000th amphibious vehicle was manufactured, Chico held a two-day celebration. In December of 1968, Randtron Incorporated acquired the plant in exchange for Randtron stock and moved production operations out of town.

Chico State College enrollment in 1950 was only 1,500, and in 1960 it was still low at 2,703 students. However, the 1970s and 1980s saw growth. The enrollment in 1971 was 10,654, and of these 1,853 were graduate students. It was renamed California State University at Chico (CSUC) in June of 1972. At this time, CSUC was located on 116 acres in downtown Chico and, in addition, had a farm of 900 acres southwest of the city. The university also began a third phase of building, which lasted over 12 years.

Butte County Community College, located between Chico and Oroville, 14 miles south of Chico, opened in September 1968. Immediately, 1,994 students enrolled. The college benefited the community, providing affordable education to residents of all ages, and vocational training opportunities as well. Enloe Hospital was able to start a Life Support System Paramedic Program in 1975, following the first paramedics' graduating class from Butte Community College in June 1974. Enrollment at Butte College increased 20 percent in 1974 and continued to rise.

The agricultural picture in the Chico area was mixed with success and challenge. In 1957, the Sutter Butte Canal Company was liquidated with four farmer-controlled districts taking its place on March 1. A special drainage district formed outside of town off State Highway 32, 1,500 feet north of the intersection between West Sacramento Avenue and Highway 32.

CHICO

There was a bumper rice crop in 1960 when 1 million bags of rice at 100 pounds each was processed at Richvale, a processing plant near Chico. The average rice yield per acre was 51 to 52 bags. The top planting occurred in 1955, which saw 80,200 acres planted. Since then, rice farmers have used allotment programs that restrict acreages planted to prevent a glut in the rice market.

The Continental Nut Company was constructed in Chico in 1960. The 45,000 square-foot building was made of steel and was located on Oleander Avenue between E. 10th and E. 11th Avenues. The company installed equipment for the bleaching and drying of English walnuts, additional grading of nuts, and the shelling and packing of nuts. It was the largest independent packer and sheller on the West Coast. Now the building houses the Chico Nut Company.

The Agricultural Extension Service of the University of California at Davis and Hugh Baber, owner of experimental cattle, did research on feeding cattle processed almond hulls. This was successful if the hulls were properly processed. The experiment was under way at the Llano Seco Ranch, outside of Chico, in 1965. It was successful and farmers still sell almond hulls to be processed for feed. Tri-County Almond, Incorporated, another Chico based nut company, acquired a 40,000-foot warehouse on a 30-acre site in Chico's Industrial Park in 1965. Mechanical orchard harvesters appeared in the early 1960s and boosted almond and walnut harvests.

Almost every crop used the mechanical harvesters once they were available; however, they were not as successful for peaches and apricots due to bruising. This did not prevent a record peach crop in 1966. They were sold at $68.50 per ton, the highest price yet.

The introduction of kiwis as a crop in Butte County, featured at the Silver Dollar Fair in May 1967, was also a big success. Farmers in Gridley began raising kiwis, and Alkop Farms produced and shipped them from Chico until they went bankrupt in the late 1990s. Jim Adams, owner of AllStar, Incorporated and former Alkop employee, purchased Alkop Farm's facilities. He now does fruit processing and cold storage. There are some locations that still produce kiwis, such as the Keefer Road Farm, which was the first grower of the fruit in the Chico area. According to Adams, they started production in 1969, and are still growing and shipping kiwis today.

A California Almond Growers Exchange receiving station opened in Chico at Miller Street, on the west side of town, in August 1967. The Agricultural Commissioners report of January 1979 placed a gross value of $161,352,700 on Butte County crop production.

Butte County's water rights were insured in an agreement with the Department of Water Resources in the 1970s. The results of the Oroville Dam were a supply of water for agricultural use in Sutter and Butte Counties. Recreationally, Lake Oroville offers 167 miles of shoreline, boating, fishing, water skiing, and camping. The Sacramento River also offers boating, fishing, and skiing, and there are many small lakes, streams, and creeks in and around Chico that local people and visitors enjoy during good weather. Bidwell Park offers golf, fishing, swimming, picnicking, and playgrounds. Plays, concerts, and special events sponsored by the city, the university, and local civic groups add to the fun and recreation available in Chico, most of which has been developed in the past 50 years.

Two events in the 1980s brought heightened awareness of historical resources within the city: a proposed two-story parking structure in the south-of-campus area and a proposal by Crocker Bank to destroy the remodeled 1901 Nottleman building downtown for additional parking. These issues galvanized a latent preservation oriented constituency and demonstrated the need for an official preservation plan. An ad hoc group of preservationists encouraged the city to adopt a preservation ordinance.

Enriching the City

Todd Radke, from the *Enterprise Record*, stated in an article written February 23, 1980: "In the past you mention historical restoration, and most people think you're talking about Independence Hall. But the transition has been realizing that history on local and state levels is just as important as national history." He went on to explain that a group called the Chico Historic Preservation Committee was born out of a dispute over the Nottleman Building at 125 W. Third Street. He pointed out the need for city council to pass historic preservation ordinances in order for whole districts and neighborhoods to be considered historic. At the time, only three buildings in Chico were considered historic: The Bidwell Mansion (1964), the Stansbury House (1977), and the Gage House (1978). Downtown Chico was still mapped out the way John Bidwell had designed it, and many buildings in that district dated back to late 1800s or early 1900s. In most instances cornices had been removed and the gingerbread was missing, but the stores often had the four original walls, or at least two or three of them.

Other historical preservation projects in 1977 included the restoration of the Stansbury House. Angeline Stansbury was the last family member to live in the house. She was 91 and lived there all of her life. The home was placed on the National Register of Historic Houses and listed in the guide to architecture in San Francisco and Northern California. James Morehead, and the City of Chico, came up with funds for the house and preserved it for Chico's sake.

The Honey Run Bridge, a covered bridge on Centerville Road built in 1894 by George Miller, was also saved by a group of concerned citizens. In 1965, the structure was 71 years old when a truck ran into the side of it, knocking an 80-foot section of the bridge into Butte Creek. The county decided the old bridge wasn't worth fixing and built a new one upstream. The State Reclamation Board demanded that someone take over the restoration of the bridge or it would be demolished. A small group of residents from Butte Creek, Honey Run Creek, Paradise, Chico, and Oroville started a "save the bridge" drive. They needed $15,000 to restore it. Finally, in 1972, the builders of the Paradise Pines Mobile Park, the Larwin Corporation from Beverly Hills, wrote a $10,000 check as a donation for the project. The money was used to purchase materials. The employees of the county worked as they had time. Construction ended September 1972. The span is now 230 feet long, the second largest bridge of its kind in the state. Mrs. Hester Patrick conducted the dedication of the Honey Run Bridge. Sheriff Larry Gillick provided one of his famous pancake breakfasts for the event, and 2,000 people attended.

Two historic sites were abandoned and left to live in people's memories only. The first was the Hotel Oaks on Second Street, between Salem and Normal, which closed permanently in October of 1966. In April 1967, the hotel was scheduled for demolition. In its place there is now a large public parking area.

Chico also had to say goodbye to its streetcar service, which was terminated in 1947. The rails were left in the downtown streets until the 1970s. The Sacramento Northern used the line down Main Street until 1977 for freight only. The streetcar operated under three different names before service was abandoned. First it was Chico Electric Company, and then it was sold to Northern Electric Company, and finally to the Sacramento Northern line. The old Chico Electric Company Depot, at East First Street and Main, was incorporated into the Sacramento Northern.

In 1983, a new plan was outlined for the Bidwell Mansion to remodel it to the historic period of 1868–1900. An archeological study of the site was conducted. The plan to reconstruct the Carriage House was initiated at the same time. Tim Simonds, a building contractor with expertise in historic restoration, rebuilt the Bidwell Mansion Carriage House at the end of the 1980s. A visitors' center was also added to the mansion grounds in the 1990s. Today, the Bidwell Mansion is a monument to Chico's heritage, and reflects the citizens' concern with preservation.

Chapter Nine

THE MODERN COMMUNITY

The integration of the university with the city of Chico balanced both and promoted growth for each of the entities. This was accomplished with Mayor Ted Meriam's supervision. He was both the chair of the board of trustees at the university and mayor for the city of Chico. He rejected the idea of too much growth too fast, for the city's sake. The university growth gave impetus to the city's 1960s desired growth plan. The university library, Meriam Library, was named in Ted's honor to show appreciation for all that he contributed to the CSUC. Ted was a collector of old books and a library enthusiast.

Chico's current economic development is looking at tourism as a viable arena for growth. The city only offers 273 hotel rooms, which is a low number in comparison with plans the city government would like to implement. The city population growth is five times the university growth today. While CSUC has been a major contributor to city growth in the past, it doesn't explain growth in the 1990s. City surveys indicate that present rate could be due to migration of people to Chico for its desirable community.

Agricultural production in modern times has dropped to approximately the 1965 level. Although production is lower, income from crops has remained level and does not indicate a drop since crops grown now are fruits and nuts that sell for a higher price. The state total for agricultural products has dropped about 40 percent overall in the last decade, while Chico income has remained constant.

For the city of Chico, great strides were made in infrastructure between 1950 and 1990. Sewer systems were upgraded and enlarged, two new fire stations were built, and a new runway and terminal were added at the airport. The Chico Parking Assessment District created three downtown parking areas for the city. The decade from 1990 to 2000 saw a 50 percent growth rate for the Chico population, which tends now to be a young population with a median age of 24.6 years. Forty-three percent of the population of Chico ranges from 24 years old or younger. Figures for population are taken from the Chico Sphere of Influence, or greater Chico, and are not representative of only the incorporated area.

For the first era ever, no major fires have destroyed downtown areas. Although city fires have been curbed, rural fires continue to be a challenge. In 1999, lightening caused numerous fires. At one point there were 47 rural fires blazing simultaneously. Chico has park fires every year, and the last big one burned 13,000 acres.

Today the Chico Fire Department is coordinated between state, county, and city. Chico was one of the last areas to coordinate in the state. Now, each fire station's response to fire depends upon whichever department is closest. It is expensive to respond to a fire, but each department covers the other areas, and the expenses balance in the end. It is called an "Automatic Aide Agreement." The state picks up the bulk of the bill for wild fire fighting, although all units in the area are involved.

Impact fees for housing development in Chico are high but helpful in maintaining a balance between development and preservation and quality of life in the city. These fees have an effect on housing prices in Chico, which are continually rising. This has made it hard for young families to buy homes. In response to this problem, low-income housing was built throughout the city. Chico was careful not to build too many units, or isolate them in one area, in order to integrate them into the community as a whole.

By 1990, Chico had a strong financial position and adequate reserves, as well as a strong annexation program. Southeast Chico and California Park, a large, modern housing development on the east side of town near Highway 32, were annexed as a redevelopment area. Other areas include the downtown and Park Avenue, grouped together into one area, and the airport. As development took place, taxes from the baseline value of the undeveloped parts of these areas, in relation to the new value after development, brought needed revenue to the city. The North Valley Plaza, the first mall in Chico, contributed to growth. It was outside of the city in the beginning, on county land, and then eventually it was annexed. In 1993, a new Chico Mall opened on 20th Street, south of town. Revenues from these developments and businesses helped with some rebuilding costs of the historic and quaint downtown, repairs of Highway 32, and the creation of bicycle paths.

Butte County was one of the original 27 counties of California. It was officially established in 1850. At that time, it included all of Plumas and parts of Sutter, Colusa, Tehama, and Sierra Counties. Even though land area has become smaller, there has been a steady growth of population, with great gains between 1850 and 1860 and again between 1940 and 1950. In the 1940s the population increased by 50 percent, and that gain seems to be consistent with present-day figures. Although the 1980 census of Chico indicates a population of 26,601, with the inclusion of the suburban area it totaled 56,000 persons. These more inclusive figures have not been reported as part of Chico until the last 30 years. Now the population sign for the city reads 100,697. This reflects the Chico Sphere of Influence, or Chico S.O.I., data.

In 1984, city council authorized a study that revealed a problem with downtown traffic. Many cars were driving through that did not have a downtown destination. This is a problem that has not been solved to this day. The city has had many obstacles to face as a modern community and is challenged today to maintain a rural atmosphere and a clean environment, as development and population grow.

Alcohol is a major problem in the city. With a student population of approximately 14,000, many come to Chico to abuse or experiment with alcohol while away from their parents. This creates a challenge for the local police. It is ironic that the Bidwells founded the town with the stipulation that imbibing alcohol was not to be permitted on their land, yet it is one of the most serious problems Chico faces at the present time. The university, and the whole downtown area, was literally Bidwell land. These two areas are the major components of the alcohol problem. Roadblock checks on Halloween, Saint Patrick's Day, and Pioneer Day have become traditions, just to curb irrational and dangerous behavior of drunken partiers.

From 1950 to 1980, the population of Chico was largely caucasian. Since 1980, the non-white portion of the population has grown and has created new challenges. According to a recent housing survey performed by the city of Chico, the non-white population is now 18 percent of the city's total population. This is a dramatic increase from 11 percent in 1990 and 6 percent in 1950. Today, a few Chinese families and individuals remain in Chico. The university draws students from all over the world, and some remain in Chico after graduating.

CHICO

There was a large influx of families from foreign countries when the Mexican braceros came across the border to work in American agricultural fields during World War II and the post-war era. In the 1950s, the bracero program in Chico allowed Mexican nationals to cross the border to work and go back at the end of the season with no penalties. Chico had 200 braceros, particularly in the rice industry. Many families that came to work, through the program, stayed in Chico as permanent residents and received their citizenship. The younger members, those under 50, are all American born and consider themselves to be "Chicoans." Today about seven percent of the population in Chico is Hispanic.

When the Vietnam War was over, Chico again experienced another large migration. Thousands of Hmong families, from Laos, came to the United States. Within the past ten years this group alone has increased their Chico population by 351 percent, climbing from 355 people to 1,602 people since 1990. Although these families were placed in large cities like Detroit, Denver, and Seattle, many eventually made their way to the California Central Valley towns of Chico, Sacramento, and Fresno, where the climate and farming conditions were similar to their homeland.

The history with the Hmong people begins with their assistance to U.S. troops in the Vietnam War. When North Vietnam won the conflict and invaded South Vietnam, the Hmong had to flee or face certain death from the new regime. They crossed the Mekong River into Thailand and lived in refugee camps until they were allowed to immigrate to the United States. Some families lived in the camps for over 11 years. The more educated and efficient refugees were taken first to the United States. Others had to wait. Eventually almost all were allowed to enter. Those who came first established communities in their new land for other Hmong people, anticipating the migration of their relatives from the refugee camps.

There were seven tribes of Hmong people, and each group had their own chiefs, but the Lee tribe was considered the leaders of them all. In Chico, Kou Lee was a leader and liaison for the Hmong people. He spoke five languages and had a masters degree in psychology, which was not recognized in this country. He secured a position as teacher's aid in the public school system. He worked at Rosedale Elementary School for several years, then transferred to Chapman Elementary School. He helped young Hmong students learn English, which he spoke fluently.

The Hmong had their own social systems. They worked as a community to pay for weddings, funerals, and college tuition. Older and more advanced students that were proficient in English went to the university, got jobs, and then worked their entire lives to allow other family members to receive an education.

Lee and some of his relatives bought land jointly on River Road and grew strawberries and other crops. The Hmong were farmers in their native land, and they continued to grow high quality fruits and vegetables in the Central Valley. The *Sacramento Bee* featured a Hmong family growing strawberries in the Sacramento area in a 2002 article. It commented on the quality of the strawberries grown by Hmong farmers because of their planting, weeding, tending, and harvesting by hand. The result was a labor-intensive crop that was high quality. The Hmong people were surprised to find that they could charge more than twice as much for their strawberries because of their farming methods, using labor instead of machinery and chemicals.

When the Hmong first began to arrive in Chico, in the late 1970s and early 1980s, the students valued their education and studied diligently. As they became "Americanized," the young people wanted to fit in with American children. Some Hmong youth got involved in gangs, and though some still focused all their interest on their studies, most began to be interested in music, clothes, and friends in addition to studying. The acculturation of the youth is now affecting the Hmong culture.

The Modern Community

Today, Hmong farmers are a large presence in the Saturday morning Farmers' Market and the Thursday Night Downtown Market in Chico. Teenagers help their parents and grandparents display and sell produce, and the small children try to amuse themselves in the booths, as families do business selling flowers, garlic, onions, greens, strawberries, tomatoes, vegetables, and other high quality goods in outdoor markets. Hmong students graduate from the school system and the university each year. Families have purchased land and are now a part of the fabric of Chico.

Meanwhile, the natives of Chico, the Mechoopda, lost 645 acres in the post–World War II era and lost their status as a tribe recognized by the federal government. They were not re-recognized as a tribe until 1992. Today Steve Santos is the elected chairman. The tribe also has a seven-member tribal council that is elected from the membership at large. Presently there are approximately 400 members of the Mechoopda Tribe, based on lineal descent. There are no fluent language speakers, but there is a small core who remember much of the language. A current priority of the Mechoopda Tribe is the acquisition of a land base again. Another high priority is the preservation of their language and knowledge of their customs, especially for the youth. A youth group is working toward reclaiming the language with regularly scheduled lessons. The Mechoopda would also like to create economic development opportunities and investments for the tribe. Due to their respect for their ancestors, the Mechoopda were working on the repatriation of their remains found in Butte County. Another issue they were tackling was the education of the community, and visitors, regarding the tribe. "If we had the resources, we would do more education at the Bidwell Mansion right now. [When Craig Henry Azbill was alive] he was a link between the tribe and the Bidwell Mansion Historic Park," Santos explains.

Carlene Conway, the first chairperson elected after the re-recognition, spent time at home, with her typewriter, doing all the work to get Mechoopda recognized by the government again. At the time, there were more issues than ever and more interaction required between the tribe and the state and federal governments. Conway says:

> Federal recognition of the Mechoopda Tribe of Chico Rancheria, also known as "the Village," took 14 years, from 1978 until 1992. It began with a makeshift office in Nice, California. In 1988 I was elected by members of the tribe to work with various agencies such as California Indian Legal Services (CILS), Bureau of Indian Affairs, and other resources to begin the process of reestablishment of our tribe. It involved many hours and years with meetings and Federal Court proceedings to get started.
>
> Our tribe formed an interim council in the beginning. We worked to draft a tribal roll, tribal constitution, by-laws and ordinances to establish funding with grants. This was to assist the tribe in getting the necessary means to get started.
>
> We now have a Community Center, which houses the administrative offices, and our Housing Corporation. The building also is used for committee meetings, Youth group activities, cultural events and many other community activities. The building is accessible to all tribal members and all other Native Americans who need assistance.
>
> Many of the Mechoopda people have begun working on the cultural regalia to start with dancing once again. There are men and women's groups involved with much determination to learn and establish our once great cultural background. One goal is to rebuild our Roundhouse.

CHICO

I would like to thank Steve Quesenberry, CILS Attorney, Bob Uliberry, and the B.I.A. and all the tribal members who have made this dream a reality. I am confident in knowing that our ancestors are proud of us all and sending their spirits to help guide our way. Wɔkten yehyeen maydə t'ikken (KonKau for "One Happy Indian, Thanks").

The Mechoopda were successful at getting reinstated and were the only tribe applying at the time that was granted all their funds. They maintain relationships with other nearby tribes. "We have a strong relationship with Grindstone. It is in the hills just outside of Chico towards the Williams/Orland area. Some years our dances are held there," Steve Santos relates.

The Mechoopda new tribal headquarters is on Mission Ranch Road, off the Esplanade in Chico. They also take an active part in the community of Chico. Steve Santos says, "Native people have always been here, and they will continue to live here and be a part of the greater community in the area. In this community, except in the early days of conflict, we have been treated pretty much like anyone else."

The Mechoopda are active in the Four Winds Charter School, a native school housed at the Fair Grounds in Chico. Private schools and charter schools have become phenomena in Chico, as in other towns in the nation. Approximately 1,100 students are home schooled in Chico each year. The public school system now must compete with high quality, viable alternatives for students.

Chico has attracted industry from other areas to establish plants or offices in town. In the past, some city government promoters would boast of affordable property and taxes and a fairly educated work force available at low wages. Chico residents wanted to change this message to business owners, in order that the Chico workforce might attain a livable wage.

Fleetwood, Incorporated, a company that manufactured trailers, was located in Chico during the 1960s and 1970s. They employed 500 people and paid a reasonable wage. They were also a profit-sharing company, which improved wages. Koret also employed 500 people and remains in business in Chico today. Aero Union presently employs over 200 people. Sierra Pacific was a large employer, but they left Chico due to the adverse affects of their industry on air quality. Unfortunately, Dandel's was so successful in Chico that they were purchased by a bigger company, and it moved the plant elsewhere. Two software companies are operating in Chico at present. Businesses have been attracted to Chico, but according to Fred Davis, former city manager, they generally do well before a bigger company buys them out and eventually relocates the business.

When the development of Chico started, all buildings and businesses were locally owned. Around the beginning of the twentieth century, outside corporations began to do business in Chico and profited from it. In the last 40 to 50 years, Chico, and other cities across the nation, have been the hosts of national corporations like Wal-Mart, Walgreen's, Target, and Homeco. In Chico, these businesses have built up largely in the southeast area. They have provided jobs and some community contributions, but overall they do not benefit the community as much as locally-owned businesses. The higher paying positions are few, most of the local employees are offered low-paying jobs, and the profits that are made by these companies are taken out of town and are not spent in Chico. Their establishment has detracted from local small business owners and has caused the closing of some local stores. They have also decentralized the business area in Chico, creating challenges in traffic and transportation.

Mixing the old with the new doesn't always work smoothly. The local newspaper closely covered the transformation of the former bank building, on Broadway and Second Street, into the new Chevy's restaurant. This was a first for Chico; nationally owned banks and a 7-11 tested the waters in Chico's downtown, but a chain restaurant had never been admitted before Chevy's. The sign for the chain restaurant was not accepted in the downtown area. The Chico Architectural Review sent Chevy's back to the drawing board. According to the article, they were not gracious about it. Somehow a compromise was reached, and Chevy's opened downtown in 1998, with a small and modest sign.

Modern day Chico has given birth to viable local industry that has employed thousands of people and provided a strong base of local economy. Chico is home of the Sierra Nevada Brewery. Ken Grossman and Paul Camusi, both California State University students, wanted to open a business in order to stay in Chico after their graduation, and in 1980 their solution was the Sierra Nevada Brewery. The result of their efforts was a popular beer that is sold nationwide. Their best-known brew is Sierra Nevada Pale Ale. The plant in Chico, located on 20th Street near the Chico Mall area, employs 300 residents and produced 566,000 barrels of beer in 2002. The first year of the company's operation, they produced 550 barrels of beer. Ken Grossman bought out his partner five years ago and is now the sole owner of the brewery.

Sierra Nevada has a strong recycling policy. Yeast and spent grain from the beer production process is delivered by Sierra Nevada employees to the university farm where it is fed to cattle, which in turn are purchased for beef that is cooked at the brewery restaurant. The company is sponsoring an experimental agricultural venture by planting a field of experimental hops near the brewery. This could prove to be a new area of agricultural production for Chico farmers if the experiment goes well. Sierra Nevada demonstrates its community consciousness in other ways, by employing and patronizing local craftsman, musicians, and artists, and by establishing a community ballroom and concert hall on their premises. The Sierra Nevada facility incorporated fine woodwork, stained glass, and other artistry in its construction, and is an extensive and attractive place. The owner is community-minded and the area is enriched by the business in many ways.

Downtown and other historic buildings in the city that were once owned by Chico residents have either been sold to people outside the area or the owners have deeded them to their heirs who have moved out of town. Residents now own only about half of downtown Chico. Preservation projects include the rebuilding of the Diamond Hotel and a movement to save the old Senator Theatre on Main Street. Many people in town would like to see the art deco style theater restored to the magnificence it once had. The Chico Heritage Association raised $10,000 in a showing of the original *Robin Hood* movie for a fundraiser called "Robin to the Rescue." This money is to be used to help restore the tower that had to be removed from the theater due to deterioration. The movie theater was a special place for Chico residents, especially those from the World War II generation. It contains WPA art deco murals and is an important example of 1930s architecture. Chicoans would like to transform it into a community performing arts center, to be "shared by the old, who have their memories, and the young, who will have their own new experience."

Chicoans appreciate newer buildings also. The Chico Area Recreation District Building won an architectural award from the American Institute of Landscape Architects of Phoenix, Arizona, in December of 1980, when it was five years old. The building is attractive and functional, designed by Hon and Ed Sue of Berkley. It provides Chico with offices, a gathering place, classroom, and a community center for senior services. It is built of redwood, glass, and stone, set in a park-like setting of trees, lawns, and walkways.

Hollywood continues to visit Chico. In 1999, *Stolen Innocence* was filmed by CBS. It was the television Movie of the Week and starred Thomas Callabro and Tracy Gold. It was filmed in downtown Chico.

CHICO

The Thunderbird Lodge, the Golden Waffle, a Chico neighborhood, the Skyway, the Cornucopia, the Honey Run Covered Bridge, and truck stops in Orland and Corning were all shot during filming. In 1996, *Ruby Ridge: An American Tragedy*, a CBS mini-series starring Laura Dern and Randy Quaid, was shot in 30 different locations including Concow, Chico, Paradise, Oroville, Orland, and Magalia.

Chico was host to a Disney Channel movie, *Under Wraps*, in 1997, about three children who find and befriend a 3,000-year-old mummy. The movie features downtown Chico, the Holly Sugar Factory in Orland, and more than a dozen other locations in Butte County.

KZFR, Chico local community radio station, started broadcasting in 1990. Erik Mathieson, who had previously worked for KPSA in Berkley, incorporated the station in 1985. He wanted to build a translator in the area. Erik has moved from Chico and now lives in Red Bluff with his wife, where they both teach high school. Before he moved, he started KZFR, 90.1 FM and a low power FM station in Oroville, KRBS 107.1. Community radio provides an opportunity for the participation and expression of many area interests over the air.

Today, single parents, mostly female, head 11 percent of all households in Chico. This is low compared with many communities in the nation. The average income for all families increased over the past decade from $19,000 to $29,000 per year. There are many choices of public, charter, and private schools, and residents tend to be well educated. Community involvement is also high because of the good weather, reportedly 311 days of the year, and the enjoyable gatherings that many civic organizations hold both outdoors and indoors in the city.

Chico residents of all ages have enjoyed the outdoor markets, the downtown concerts in the plaza on Friday evenings during the spring and summer months, and other events sponsored by the Chico Downtown Business Association.

The entire picture is not positive, however. A task force was formed in Chico to address youth-related gang problems with Southeast Asian, Mexican, and African-American youth. Recent struggles include the shooting and wounding of a police officer by a gang member from a neighboring community in 2003 in Chico. Gang issues are primarily related to racial identity, territory, and drug sales. Gang members are a small percentage of people in the community, but they do impact the quality of life.

Chico lifestyle is enviable. The city of Chico was in the right place at the right time, and its history is rich and complex. There will always be something new and interesting to learn about Chico—the city has been fortunate. To have the Mechoopda settle on the banks of the creeks in the Chico area was advantageous. John Bidwell's interest in the location was fortuitous. Chico has been the focus of national attention in ways that have benefited the city growth many times.

It is rumored that Dr. Newton Enloe pawned his watch to start Enloe Hospital. Annie Bidwell placed the Bidwell Park lands in trust, and out of her hands in 1910, in case she would be "tempted to sell" the property to meet expenses before her death. These types of unselfish actions by many Chico citizens have increased the city's fortune. The discovery of gold; almond orchards; duck hunting; Warner Brothers and the U.S. Feature Film Company of 1914; the Honey Run Bridge; Shakespeare in the Park; the North Valley Plaza; Chief Tovee; The Chico Colts; the Greenline; The Mechoopda "Big Time" celebration; and the Coot are all part of the story of Chico, and Chico's fortune.

The Bidwells went into debt to foster the community and gifted the city with one of the largest parks in America. The Mechoopda sacrificed all their land. Countless citizens have served the area by giving countless hours of their time to create, protect, and preserve. The community has worked to make Chico a City of Fortune today.

BIBLIOGRAPHY

Books

Clough, Frederick S. *The House on 5th and Salem*. Chico: Stansbury Home Preservation Association, undated.

Diller, J.S. *Guidebook of the Western United States, Part D. The Shasta Route and Coast Line*. United States Geological Survey, Department of the Interior, 1915.

Dixon, Rolland B. *Maidu Texts*. Lyden, Holland: E.J. Brill,1912.

———. *The Northern Maidu*. New York: AMS Press, 1905.

Heizer, Robert F. *The Destruction of the California Indians*. Nebraska: University of Nebraska Press, 1974.

Hendrix, Louise Butts. *Sutter Buttes Land of Histum Yani*. Marysville, CA: Normart Printing Company, 1985.

Hill, Dorothy. *The Indians of the California Rancheria*. California: California Department of Parks and Recreation, 1978.

Hodges, Terry. *Sabertooth, Rip-Roaring Adventures of a Legendary Game Warden*. Boulder, CO: Paladin Press, 1988.

Hust, Stephen G. *This is My Own, My Native Land*. Yuba City, CA: Independent Press, 1956.

Hutchinson, W.H. *One Man's West*. Chico: Hurst and Yount, 1948.

Lassen, Rene Weybye. *Uncle Peter: The Story of Peter Lassen and the Lassen Trail*. Paradise, CA: Ox Shoe Publications, 1990.

Magliari, Michael F. and Michael J. Gillis. *John Bidwell and California, The Life and Writings of a Pioneer 1841–1900*. Spokane, WA: The Arthur H. Clark Company, 2003.

Mansfield George C. *History of Butte County, California with Biographical Sketches*. Los Angeles: Historic Record Company, 1918.

McGie, Joseph F. *History of Butte County, Volume 1 (1840–1919)* and *Volume 2 (1920–1980)*. Oroville, CA: Butte County Board of Education, 1982.

O'Hare, Carol, ed. *How I Learned to Ride the Bicycle: Reflections of a 19th Century Woman, Frances E. Willard*. Sunnyvale, CA: Fair Oaks Publishing, 1991.

Ortiz, Bev. *It Will Live Forever*. Berkley, CA: Heyday Books, 1991.

Powers, Stephen. *Tribes of California*. Berkley, CA: University of California Press, 1976.

Stephens, Kent. *Matches, Flumes and Rails, The Diamond Match Company in the High Sierra*, First Edition. Corona Del Mar, CA: Trans-Anglo Books, 1981.

Swett, Ira, ed. *Sacramento Northern*. Los Angeles: Interurbans Electric Railways Publications, 1962.

Talbitzer, Bill. *Butte County*. Northridge, CA: Windsor Publications, Inc., 1987.

Wells, Harry L. *History of Butte County*. San Francisco: Harry L. Wells, 1882.

Wilson, Neill C. and Frank J. Taylor. *Southern Pacific: The Roaring Story of a Fighting Railroad*. New York: McGraw Hill, 1952.

CHICO

Articles, Interviews, Periodicals, and Miscellaneous

Bidwell, John. "Echoes of the Past, State of California." *The Century Magazine*.

Resources Department, Department of Parks and Recreation (March 1987).

Brilts, Juri G. "Save the Senator!" California State University, Office of Sponsored Programs (June 5, 2003).

Butte County Aviation Historical Society. *Air Born*. (video), June 1994.

Chico City Library. *Annual Reports*. 1954–1956.

Chico High School Yearbooks. Personal Collections. 1911–1920.

Chico Visitor Guide. Chico: Chico News and Review and Chico Chamber of Commerce, 2001.

City of Chico. *Annual Reports*. 1954–1996.

City of Chico. *Chico City Council Publications*. 1954–1959.

City of Chico. *City of Chico General Plan*. 1994.

The Colombia Gazetteer of North America. 2000. http://www.bartleby.com/69/S00253.html.

Davis, Fred. Former Chico City Manager. Interview. Chico: April 7, 2003.

Deter, Darrell. Chico Museum Association. Interview. Chico: April 22, 2003.

"Folly of a Life of Crime." *The Diggins* 3.21 (1977)

Gallardo, John. President Chico Heritage Association. Interview. Chico: February 12, 2003.

Hicks, Michael. Chico Business Owner. Interview. Chico: June 12, 2003.

"History of the Delta." *Interactive Guide to the San Joaquin Delta*. 2003. http://www.sacdelta.com/hist.html.

King, Robbins and Mary King. Interviews. Chico: January 17, 2003.

Kroeber, A.L. Handbook of the Indians of California, Bulletin 78, Washington, D.C.: Smithsonian Institute, Bureau of American Ethnology, government Printing Office, 1925.

Livingston, Matthew. Railroad Collector. Interview. Chico: November 1, 2002.

Marino, Carrie E. "Robin Hood Slept Here." *Butte County Senior Post* May 1993.

Mathews, Frances. Interview. Chico: December 12, 2002 and January 30, 2003.

Meriam, Chip and Doris McLean Meriam. Interview. Chico: May 8, 2003.

Meriam, Theodore. "My Home Town." Public Address. Chico: January 17, 1993.

———. "One Hundred and Eight Years of Oser's." Public Address. Chico: October 19, 1986.

Needham, Mick. Chico Business Owner. Interview. Chico: June 30, 2003.

"The Nome Cult Walk: In Memory of Gaylan Azbill." *Round Valley Reservation*. 2002. http://www.covelo.net/tribes_nome_cult.html.

Nopel, John. Chico Historian. Interview. Chico: April 23, 2003.

Orberg, George. "The Chinese in Chico." *The Diggins* 4.3 (1960).

Sacramento Valley League Publications. Personal Collections. 1936–1951.

Sands, Tony and Ann Sands. Interview. March 8, 2003.

Santos, Steve, Chairman of the Mechoopda Tribe. Interview. Chico: December 23, 2002 and March 8, 2003.

Sigel, Ann. Interview. January 30, 2003.

Stewart, Elizabeth, Chico Heritage Association. Interview. Chico: February 10, 2003.

Selected clippings: *Normal Record. Chico Record. Chico Enterprise. Chico Enterprise Record. Chico News and Review. Chico Examiner. Sacramento Bee*. Collections: Chico Heritage Association Archives, Butte County Library Archives, and Personal Collections, 1914–2003.

INDEX